A
GREEN
TOO FAR

By the same author
The Gathering Bunker

A GREEN TOO FAR

Golfing Adventures

Kevin Pakenham

LITTLE, BROWN AND COMPANY

A *Little, Brown* Book

First published in Great Britain in 1997
by Little, Brown and Company

Copyright © 1997 by Kevin Pakenham

A CIP catalogue record for this book
is available from the British Library.

ISBN: 0 316 64169 3

Typeset in Plantin by Solidus (Bristol) Ltd
Printed and bound by Clays Ltd, St Ives plc.

Little, Brown and Company (UK)
Brettenham House
Lancaster Place
London WC2E 7EN

To my brother Michael, golfer but diplomat.

Contents

Clubs and Hearts   1

The Perfect Weight   25

A Better Mousetrap   41

The Root of Success   63

The Secretary Goes Ex   87

To Westbourne and Back   105

Single-minded   127

Don't Send a Boy   149

The Old Heave-ho   171

Clubs and Hearts

I had never thought of women as being especially forgiving, so when Celia's mother rang me, saying that Celia would like a reconciliation, I was suspicious. It was like being given a four-footer at the sixth: you knew it was done to stop you getting practice, so that when the pressure came on the later holes you'd fluff it.

But things had been rather dreary at home without Celia. After my débâcle at the final of the Captain's Cup, my relationship with golf had undergone a sea-change. Never 'confident morning again', rather the bitter struggle with the demon of the green, the awful purgatory of the ageing golfer.

'I've decided to join Lake Park,' said Celia one Saturday morning over the cornflakes some weeks after our reconciliation. I had no complaints to make about her return. She seemed to have lost a little weight while staying with her mother, but she was quickly putting it on again and getting back her rosy cheeks. We had slipped rapidly into the old routine, like a comfortable pair of bedroom slippers (if somewhat worn), and I was psyching myself up for the day's golf, presuming that my gentle lady was doing the same vis-à-vis the dreaded mulching, spiking and turning of the unforgiving sod.

3

'Splutter,' I replied, if you see what I mean. 'Not dear old Lake Park! Bust four times. Trying again, is it? Anyway, it's a golf club, dear.'

'I know it's a golf club, James. I *can* play, if you remember.'

'You're not planning to play with me?' I asked, aghast. I was staggered and not, I have to admit, over-joyed.

'Don't worry, dear Jim, not with you. I just think we need to have something in common.'

My heart sank. She had understood nothing. Golf is not a game that you have in common with anyone. It is a personal burden that we take with us to the grave. But I am being maudlin. At that moment I would rather have heard Celia being positive about some-thing than spend my days alone. I had to admit that I had, in particular, missed her work in the garden. I had set up a golf net there in my first enthusiasm, but now I rather wished she would put her hand to the garden again. Golf for her was a second best, in my view.

'Good show, old sport.' I choked it out.

She looked at me with what I would have described in a man as wry humour, but I suppose in her case you would call it an old-fashioned look.

'It's not just a golf club, you know. It's a country club.'

'A what?'

A nasty suspicion was lurking in my mind. She illuminated it. 'Really, James, you know perfectly well. Dining facilities, indoor pool, aerobics and modern dance courses, with on-site fitness monitoring, sauna, steam, squash. And what I'm told is really popular is the dinner dance organised by the Ballroom Dance Society every Wednesday and Saturday.'

I stared into the cornflakes. I could have wept.

I was playing with Bob that morning, not a bad fellow if you can put up with pipe-smoking and bad temper. He was prepared to be sympathetic, if in a rather back-handed way.

'There's a perfectly good ladies' section at Wilfrid's. I really can't see why anyone should want to play anywhere else. I'll tell Celia so myself.' He gave his feet a good stamp.

This was not a line I really wished to encourage.

'Oh, I wouldn't do that. Her mind's quite made up. Anyway, I suppose she's more interested in the dining and ballroom dancing. She's just trying to show her enthusiasm for a common interest.'

'Sounds rum to me. I'd have thought there were better places than Lake Park, not just for golf but for almost anything.' He swished the five iron he was holding through a dandelion head.

'At least it's all in one place.' I began to feel defensive on Celia's behalf.

'Convenience shopping, eh?'

'Something like that.'

It had been a rather desultory foursome, and Bob and I were waiting for our respective partners to drive from the fourteenth. One of the great joys of St W's is that a foursome can jump down the fairways by cutting across the sandhills while waiting for your partner's drive. We had been here rather a long time.

'No sign of either of their drives, is there?' asked Bob.

The truth was that the ghastly contemplation of Lake Park had driven our own round out of our minds.

'Hold it,' I said. 'I think I can see Arthur waving.'

'They can't both have topped them!' exclaimed Bob.

But they had, and we had to trudge back to the tee.

Only over the frothing bitter, pride of St Wilfrid's, did Bob return to our conversation.

'I wouldn't let my wife join Lake Park. I don't suppose I'd see her again.'

'You should have more faith in the fair sex, even at Lake Park,' I countered.

'Oh, I don't suppose it's so bad,' said Arthur, looking blankly into his golden brew. He had that vacant gaze that was so familiar after a bruising at St W's.

'Of course it's so bad, old boy. I wouldn't touch it

with a bargepole,' roared Bob, prodding the end of his pipe at Arthur.

Arthur looked further put down, his sad good looks sadder than ever. I seemed to remember he had lost his wife to some chap from Peastings, down the coast. Touchy subjects are not the stuff of proper club conversation, not at St Wilfrid's, anyway. Arthur ran his hand through his jet-black but slightly thinning hair. I came to his rescue.

'I don't think you or your bargepole would be in the least bit welcome at Lake Park, my dear Bob,' I said. 'Let's just draw a veil over the whole place.'

'Quite so,' said Bob, laughing. 'We've polluted the air enough already.'

There's something about a new golf course that gets under the skin. I don't mean the half-finished tees and all the sand on the greens; I mean the embarrassing optimism, that awful sense of misplaced hope that shuffles around the plaster-smelling, concrete-floored changing-rooms and releases itself with a dull hiss into the members' bar.

'How was it, dear?' I asked Celia as she came in from her afternoon at Lake Park, her cheeks throbbing with their rosy tint.

'Joyous.'

'Joyous?'

'Don't ask, if you're going to be rude.'

'Well, don't say it's joyous.'

'Why not?'

'It can't be, dear. No new course can be joyous. Promising perhaps, even exhilarating, but joyous? Never.'

'Would you pour me a drink, please, James?'

So you see what I mean when I describe the brave – in the French sense – mien of the members of the new club. They hit the ball across the bulldozed swamp, carpet-weed heavy on their shoes, and chip from lush growth a few feet from the green onto steam-rollered flats, green-sprayed to disguise their origins. And within their little hearts beats a frenzied hope, a poor flame flickering in a hostile world, that one day this sorry track will be one of the great courses of England; no, Europe; no, the World, the Universe!

The following weekend I was playing with Arthur in the monthly medal, a somewhat tedious round made more so by his new-found interest in different types of grass, with which he regaled me in counterpoint to our indifferent efforts.

'Why the hell are you so interested in grass all of a sudden?' I asked as we trampled in the lush stuff mixed with wild flowers to the left of the seventeenth. It took him a while to answer, but when he did I was embarrassed for him.

'As a matter of fact, I'm rather good on grass.'

Golfers say all sorts of silly things while looking for their balls, so I ignored this. But I was stupid enough to bring it up again over a golden pint in the bar.

'So what's all this about grass, Arthur?'

'Oh, nothing, really.' He drew on the foaming brew. 'I'm just giving a helping hand.'

'With grass?'

'Yes.'

'Of course.'

We sat in silence. I knew there was something going on. I waited.

'The thing is,' he said, digging his hand into the packet of crisps he had been fighting to open, 'I'm rather good with grass.'

'You certainly took enough on the eighth.'

'I was asked to help.'

'Who by?'

'Someone I met.'

'For goodness' sake, Arthur, spit it out. What on earth's going on?'

It was a straight question and he answered with relief in his voice.

'Since you're so inquisitive, I'll tell you. I've been asked to help on their choice of grass at Lake Park.'

It was grotesque. Here was Arthur, a perfectly good member of a perfectly good club attached to a great course, no less, and there he was advising on the grass at Lake Park. I sighed and looked at the bubbles rising slowly from the remains of my pint. He too was growing inert.

'It was Miriam Fry, actually.'

Miriam Fry, eh? Celia's NBF, or New Best Friend. The two had become friendly during our little separation, and no doubt Miriam had regaled Celia with her modern views, not that I thought they sat very well with Celia's innate sense of what is right. To be quite honest, I couldn't see why they went on being friends now that I was back on the scene.

'What's Miriam Fry got to do with it?'

'She's Lady Treasurer this year, and quite a force in the land.'

'She used to be a member here.'

'She says this club is for wimps.'

'So be it,' I said with some hauteur, showing my desire not to pursue this trivial bandying with words. Unwilling to show my contempt for poor Arthur, I smiled thinly into my diminishing pint.

'There's no point in being so sniffy about it, Jim. All golf clubs have to begin somewhere.'

'I couldn't disagree more. Most golf clubs should never have begun at all.'

'Not everyone can play Wilfrid's, you know.'

'Do be serious, Arthur. Most people have neither the physical nor mental capacity to play anywhere and,' I added with magisterial conviction, 'they shouldn't try.'

★

As I dozed off in front of the ten o'clock news that evening I felt at peace with the world, with myself, even with Celia, as she brought me a cup of hot chocolate to ease my pleasantly tired bones in preparation for bed.

'Well, you do seem to have had a good day. You're positively purring, dear.'

'Yes, it was rather fun. Arthur's not such a bad old stick really.'

'You must have beaten him.'

'Maybe.' I smiled. 'By the way, he says he's involved in grass. He must be losing his marbles.'

'Well, he's quite the hero of Lake Park. He probably told you.'

'I try to ignore the afflictions of my friends.'

'Well, Miriam Fry likes him.'

'Not *the* Miriam Fry?' I said, somewhat disingenuously.

'They're the toast of the mixed fourballs.'

'What does Mr Fry think?'

'I'm sure it's all perfectly innocent. After all, it was innocent when you used to play with her, or so you said.'

'It certainly was.'

'Well, I'm sure it is with Arthur. She's a happily married woman.'

'How disgusting. I'm going to bed before you give

11

me nightmares.' I like to tease Celia a little occasionally.

We all have nightmares, and birthdays for that matter, and in my experience the only thing worse than my own birthday is Celia's. This probably goes for the fair sex in general, and the conquering fair sex in particular. A wife's birthday is an event of unequalled horror, rightly regarded by husbands much as the maiden aunts regarded the Roman Saturnalia. It is the one day in the year when the proper order of things is reversed and no request is too dreadful to refuse. So it was with Celia.

'James, dear, have you any plans for next Saturday?'

The sheer effrontery of the question took my breath away, so much so that I almost inhaled the buttered parsnip that I was carefully projecting towards my open jaws.

'None in particular. What inspires thee, my lady?' I felt fine words would be a defence.

'Nothing inspires me. I just wondered if you had made any plans.'

Was this a subtle ruse to turn my flank and force me to admit I had forgotten her birthday, or to smoke out my plans so that she could change them? It proved to be the latter.

'Of course I've got plans, my buttercup. Your mother would never have forgiven me.'

'Well, cancel them. I have better ones. You've heard of a birthday surprise? Well, this time it's going to be my surprise to you.'

One-two-three, one-two-three, one. Pause. One-two-three, one-two-three, one. Pause, and maybe lift, for all I know. The lights – chandeliers, no less – were bright, the music rum-pom-pom, the men saturnine in the main, though with flashes of asinine, and the women a swirling mass of shining, bulging satin, taffeta and acrylic, a mesmeric whole into which Celia and I, not daring to protest, were drawn.

It was music night, or ballroom dance night, or Celia's glorious anniversary by any other name. Of course, I knew perfectly well what I was in for as I sat in the back seat, blindfolded, for her birthday treat. I had easily worked out the full horror of it, a chance to relive the ballroom dancing days of our early marriage, which had happily atrophied under the demands of our more serious middle-aged addictions.

'You dance very well, Jim,' said Miriam. The music was slow and her mouth was almost touching my ear.

'There's really no problem, not if you can hit a decent three wood from the fairway,' I said modestly. 'It's just a matter of one half of your body going forward to one rhythm, while another part of your body is going backwards to another rhythm.'

'Oh, I've never thought of it like that.'

'I seem to remember you had a very good swing rhythm.'

'I meant dancing.'

Once you've spent a lot of time on a golf course with someone, man or woman, you've seen them with their defences down, in their moment of ultimate weakness, however well disguised, and you have to feel some lingering sympathy for them, however misplaced. So I felt for Miriam, my mixed foursome partner of an earlier time, as we stepped from the dance floor to our table by the plush gold, red and green curtains of the Lake Park ballroom.

'You two were dancing beautifully,' Celia greeted us.

'Yes,' agreed Arthur.

'Oh, thank you.' Miriam smiled rather sweetly. 'Jim was saying it was just like golf.'

Celia's and Arthur's laughs were somehow insulting.

'There's no doubt that a good golfer will always be able to master ballroom dancing,' I said. 'Miriam is living proof.'

'Well, I'm glad you've said so, because Arthur's suggested a little competition,' said Celia in saccharine tones.

'Oh, really? Spit it out, old pal,' I rejoined.

Perhaps the mood of the place and the odd glass of wine were having some effect.

'Well, I thought it would be fun for Miriam and I to take on you and the birthday girl.'

'What a splendid idea,' I gushed. 'Are you on, Miriam?'

'On what?'

'Ballroom dancing, of course,' I said with confidence.

'No, actually not,' whined Arthur, or anyway in retrospect it sounded like a whine. 'Golf.'

'Golf!' I repeated on a slightly lower note. 'Golf. Hmm. Golf. I didn't think you felt that enthusiastic about St Wilfrid's, dear.'

'Not that zoo for dinosaurs?' asked Miriam.

You get the idea, an ill-assorted group, perhaps a little merry, tongues wagging loosely, silly things being said.

'Steady on, dear lady,' I said, as light-heartedly as I could manage.

'Well, I do think it would be fun to see you pit your wits against Lake Park.' Celia looked intent.

I had rapidly sobered up, not just at Miriam's slur on the old club, but with an awful foreboding as to what was to follow on this special day, Celia's birthday, on which her wishes could not be lightly refused.

'We're teeing off at nine-fifteen, here, mixed foursomes, you and I against Miriam and Arthur. My real birthday present, dear.'

It is a truth, universally acknowledged, that a husband-and-wife golf team, once formed, is on its way to divorce. I felt trapped. Was this to be the final

15

blow dealt to my recently revived marriage by Celia herself, with her two friends willing accomplices in our collective downfall?

'Don't you think it might be better to split the partners up?' I asked diffidently. 'Though of course, dear, I'd love to play with you.'

'Miriam and Arthur are hardly partners, old thing. Mr Fry *is* alive and well. And they've entered for the Lake Park Mixed Foursomes, so they must practise together.'

'Anyway,' purred Miriam, 'you'll love Lake Park, whoever you play with.'

The first tee was everything I most dreaded – the blades of grass, the sand uneven like dandruff amidst the broken divots, the brand-new tee markers and the huge board carefully painted with a grotesque plan of Hole One: the green luminous green, the bunker sand the colour of corn and the stream a brilliant blue. All quite unlike the real scrubby outlook on which we had to play.

'Boys away,' said Miriam with a cheery chirrup, which stung like Dettol on my sore head.

'You're up,' said Celia.

'Rightyho!' said Arthur, trying to loosen his painfully stiff back.

The wind was strong enough to make the drive onto the wide fairway more complex than you might imagine. I had reconciled myself to the fade of middle years, but it did sacrifice distance, and the brook (or burn, as the course planner had it) threaded its way upwards from near left to far right.

It was a badly designed hole. With the uphill and the brook it took a 200-yard carry to clear the brook in the middle of the fairway, and with fade it put the carry at 220. You could play short, but that would really make the hole too easy.

To cut a long story short, I hit it into the brook. Actually, to cut a very long story short, it was that sort of course. Play short of the hazards and it was really no test of golf at all. Play a proper club, and in you went with tedious certainty. And thanks to the general level of play, it was not only a nightmare at Lake Park, but a nightmare at Lake Park in slow motion.

Celia was really rather a good sport about it all.

'Terribly sorry, darling,' I apologised, 'I just seem to find trouble wherever I hit.'

'Don't worry, dear, so long as you're enjoying it.'

'Oh, I am, I am.'

'It's a very pretty course, isn't it?'

'Oh yes, dear, very pretty.'

'I'm so glad you've played it once.'

This raised my spirits somewhat.

Relations between the other couple were not so cordial; in fact, I found it quite annoying. I knew Arthur wasn't a great golfer, but Miriam was really laying into him, and they were one up. I wondered what she would say if they were losing.

As it happened, they did fall behind on the fifteenth. Standing on the barren tee, on which a gibbet would not have seemed out of place, one looked up a hill towards a low rampart crowned, 160 yards off, by a red triangle. In a word, a dull and scrofulous hole redeemed by only one thing: we won it.

Arthur put the ball up to the flag and I would have thought it would be stiff. Fortunately the green had been imported in sections from pieces of the M25 and the ball soared off, bounding over into the hawthorn beyond and below.

'You might at least look for it,' rasped Miriam.

'We're doing our best,' I protested from the thicket.

'I don't mean you, Jim, I mean my partner.' I could see her point. It never does to openly insult the opposition; more tact is required on that front.

'It's bloody thick in here,' spluttered Arthur, a thin trickle of shrub falling from above his left eye. I saw Miriam's reasoning, because his head was no longer engaged in the task but was trapped at an awful angle amidst the climbing briars.

'You shouldn't have put it there.'

I felt quite annoyed for my friend.

'You shouldn't make the greens of cement.'

'You shouldn't play here if it's too difficult for you.' She did her best to smile as she engaged me in

18

repartee. I realised we had never before played on opposing sides, and memories of our victory so cruelly denied hovered.

'Let me give you a hand,' broke in Celia sweetly. 'It may have hopped right over.'

Luckily it had, so cutting off a descent into bitterness. The ball was just playable but Miriam conceded without a shot. She seemed to be getting in an awful state, further reminder of how we failed at the Lady Captain's Prize.

Standing on the next tee, Arthur put his arm round Miriam's shoulder.

'Awfully sorry about that, my dear. Wrong club.'

She shook him off rather brusquely. Her emotional control had not improved since our partnership. I was rather unnerved by her behaviour, but felt I should stand up for the honour of St W's.

'Your shot was perfect, Arthur. In my opinion, the green was unplayable.'

'His shot might have made do at clubs of an earlier time, but at a proper modern club it was simply inadequate,' Miriam enunciated with clarity.

I breathed in deeply. Celia took my hand.

'It's our honour, Jim.'

Well, we took the lead at the next and were dormy to the last, another field, this time downhill. It was, however, improved by a large basin of black plastic half-filled with stagnant, slime-covered water, which guarded the green, a veritable Sargasso.

'Very picturesque,' I ventured as we stood to play our two approaches, Arthur and I, 150 yards or thereabouts from the green. I hit a beaut, as the antipodeans would have it, but it rolled over the back into a clump of dock leaves. Arthur had to crack it over onto the green to save the match.

'Don't leave it short,' said Miriam helpfully.

'Definitely not short,' I added.

The sympathetic magic worked; he took a shade of earth before the ball and, with a weak trajectory, it looped into the Stygian depths.

There are few pleasures so unsullied as to witness the disastrous shot played by your opponent on the eighteenth. In any normal circumstances I would have smiled inwardly, perhaps even bitten my lip to avoid any outward display of pleasure. But the circs were far from normal. I can honestly say that my heart bled for my fellow golfer, fellow human being, fellow member of St Wilfrid's.

'*No!*' It was a wail, a shriek. 'How *could* you?' Miriam cried.

'I'm so sorry, Miriam,' sniffled Arthur.

'Don't bother to apologise.'

She turned her back on him, holding the handle of her motorised trolley as if to draw strength from the lethal object. Then she rounded on Arthur and came out with an astonishing statement.

'And I thought you Wilfridians could play. Take your airs and graces somewhere else. You're all as — ' – and I leave blank the word she used – 'as each other.'

I think you will agree that at this point she had over-stepped the realms of good taste.

'Well, if that's the way you feel,' I said, 'we might as well walk in.'

Celia was quite equable. 'I think we should at least finish the game. It is, after all, my birthday treat.'

'Of course, dear. After all, a game of golf is a game of golf, whatever the circumstances.'

I felt rebuked and I had forgotten this golden prin-ciple in the heat of the occasion. Once more I con-trolled my temper with the greatest difficulty. What was the matter with Miriam? I asked myself.

'I'm relieved to see the ancient tendency has not entirely lost its manners,' Celia added with a laugh. I don't quite know what she was laughing at, but certainly Miriam striding out towards the black-plastic morass with poor Arthur stumbling after her, and Miriam's trolley whirring along out front, was more than a little bizarre. We had not yet seen the half of it.

'You hold the trolley, partner, and I'll fish out the ball,' hissed Miriam when they reached the artificial marshland.

'Certainly, Miriam, of course.'

He was very flustered and understandably upset, but a man of his experience should have been able to

21

grasp the rudiments of an electric trolley. I suppose he held on when he should have let go, or vice versa.

He tried to steer it on the pebbled path round the edge, began to spin the offside wheel, lurched off the path onto the steeply sloping bank and gravity took over. The engine stopped with a hiss as the battery hit the watery crudescence, but Arthur went on struggling, slipping and sliding on the uneven bottom of the pond as he tried to regain his stance, a sort of drunken tap-dance in slow motion occasionally enlivened by a complete lateral body movement, leading to his disappearance beneath the murky – if threshing – waters, until once more he rose like a distressed hippopotamus from its disturbed repose.

It was the saddest end to a game of golf I've ever experienced, and I felt nothing but remorse as I drove Celia home.

'Well,' she said, 'you certainly see people's true character on the golf course.' She seemed in surprisingly good spirits.

'Quite so,' I said. 'Poor old Arthur.'

'But what about Miriam? Did you know she was like that?'

'Oh, she was always like that, too much emotion to be a real golfer.'

'She's always been like that?'

'Yes, always.'

'And you think her behaviour was acceptable, on a

golf course?' asked Celia with a little frown.

'Of course not,' I replied firmly.

Celia smiled contentedly and put her hand on my knee, a most surprising end to a day I would rather not relive. Why Celia had enjoyed it so much, and what had driven her to arrange the whole thing in the first place, I could not fathom.

The postscript was no less peculiar.

A few days later I received a copy of a letter of complaint from the Secretary of Lake Park to the Secretary of St Wilfrid's. Apparently the motorised trolley belonged to Lake Park and Miriam Fry had implicated me in its abuse.

'Good God, Celia, whatever are that club of yours and that woman up to now?'

'Let me see, dear.'

I passed the letter across the muesli, a recent innovation of Celia's.

She perused it swiftly. 'I wouldn't take any notice, dear,' she said and tore the letter into pieces.

'That's rather bold. Won't there be trouble at Lake Park?'

'Not over this, there won't.'

'Why on earth not?'

'Didn't I tell you? It's gone into receivership again.' She said it with surprising levity.

I could not be so light-hearted. Be it ever so

unprepossessing, a golf course is still a golf course, and I had striven with my whole being that Sunday morning to master it. Sad indeed that nature in all its barbarism would wrest back from the hand of man the promise of civilisation that a new golf course represents. But perhaps I'm being emotional.

The Perfect Weight

There is something infinitely satisfying about a perfectly weighted golf shot. The ball seems to roll with purpose, yet unhurried, landing softly but firmly, or, if a putt, keeping its line to the required degree, purring as if nudged by a finely tuned motor to its appointed place.

'That'll be awfully close, whatever happens' is the sort of remark that follows the perfectly weighted mid-iron. 'It always looked in' denotes the perfectly weighted putt.

This interest in perfect weightedness is common to all golfers, but occasionally it spills over into another rather bitter aspect of the game of golf.

'Perfectly weighted? You make me laugh. You're about as well weighted as an elephant.'

'I wasn't talking about myself. I was talking about my shot,' Johnny Douglas said defensively.

I was being a little harsh, perhaps, but Johnny, my current golf partner, had shown a tendency to swell and had bored us all with his efforts to contain his girth. Johnny and I had played together off and on for many a good year, and an inferiority complex he certainly did not suffer from, either concerning golf or ladies. In fact, he had been rather keen on Celia once, but I'd seen to that – I'd married her. But this thing about his weight was new.

'No spuds, please, I'll just have the salad.'

'Who are you trying to fool? Some lady out there, I suppose, eh?'

'No, actually I'm just feeling a bit porky.'

'Well,' I replied, looking him over while others pushed past the DIY lunch bar, 'I do see what you mean, but it never did a swing any harm.'

'You're so wrong, it does the greatest damage. It constricts the body turn and leads you to turn just your shoulders,' said Johnny with rather a lot of heat.

'I can see that sticking out your rear end may require rather an effort, and not be very elegant besides, but something like that must take second place to golf.'

I had piled my plate high with freshly cut, honey roast ham, tongue in aspic and some pink beef, surrounded by an ensemble of baked potato (large), beetroot, lettuce and neatly balanced dollops of mayonnaise – just the thing to prepare one for a plate of fruit cake and Stilton before the coffee and kümmel; a reasonable hors d'oeuvre to the afternoon round.

'That's pathetic,' I said, sneering at his lettuce leaf and half-slice of ham. 'And I suppose you won't have any of Dundee's contribution to civilisation?' I referred of course to the fruit cake.

'Correct,' he replied, with the sort of strangled pomposity one imagines coming from a Spartan hero, or a fat golfer on a slimming kick.

'What is it, Johnny, old chap? We like you the way you are,' I said over the kümmel.

'Or at least we wouldn't like to take the chance on any experiments,' added Bob in his charitable way.

'Put a sock in it, can't you? I told you, I feel a bit porky,' Johnny said lamely.

The fact was that before his slimming kick he looked much like the rest of us. What the French call Roast Bif, I believe. I couldn't see what his problem was. Still, he played damn well that afternoon. Despite his diminishing girth, Johnny hit the ball with distance and authority, well weighted, no less.

At the end of the round he turned to us and said, 'By the way, chaps, a friend of mine is going to join me for lunch next Saturday, and,' he hurried on, 'she would like to walk round afterwards.'

We are of course a broad-minded lot and we had all encountered this sort of thing before. Indeed, it is part of the spirit of St Wilfrid's to humour the female interest, even when connected to golf. It's always a pleasure to have someone to admire one's shots.

'Good show,' Bob said with a straight face, and Harry and I concurred.

The next Saturday was a beautiful clear day, typical of early autumn. The wind was a mere breeze up the Channel and only when we mounted the fourth tee did we feel the salty zephyr freshen our inner being.

'Difficult to know whether to wear a pullover or not,' remarked Bob.

'It's the time of year,' I said. 'Clout casting in reverse, if you see what I mean.'

'Nonsense. It's invigorating, that's all,' said Johnny. He threw out his chest and whirled the club round his head in preparation for his agonisingly inelegant swing.

'You'll get awfully cold if you don't put on at least something,' I said with quite unnecessary concern, a build-up to my next remark. 'After all, you don't have the covering you used to.'

'Do you think so?' asked Johnny with real interest. Bracing back his shoulders, he added, 'In any case, warmth is simply a question of a healthy circulation, not fat, unless you're some kind of seal.'

Johnny was in something of a showing-off mood, which was reinforced at lunch. (Actually, I never discourage that sort of a thing in an opponent.) Miss Josie Rafter had arrived and he was squiring her round the dining-room like an owner at Cruft's. She did look rather like a poodle, with her frizzy hair and a little pink ribbon in it. Eventually we were all seated and I turned the conversation to the afternoon round.

'It'll probably get rather nippy towards the end of the round. There's always a wind at Wilfrid's and at this time of the year it can get awfully cold by five-thirty.'

'Quite so, Jim. You hear that, Josie? It's good advice. Wrap up warm.'

'You should have seen Johnny this morning, impervious to the wind. You'll have to wear something a little more than a shirt this afternoon, old man,' I added helpfully.

'Arrant nonsense. You know, Josie, these chaps are getting frail in their old age. Once, long ago, Jim would hardly have worn a t-shirt in midwinter – if they were allowed, that is. Now his poor arteries are furring up, so he goes out in three layers of jersey.'

'Oh, did you really, Mr South?'

'Call me Jim.'

'Rather forward, aren't you, Jim? The poor girl's not used to such informality. Not the sort of thing you get in a solicitors' office, is it, Josie?'

'Oh, Johnny, you do tease me so,' Josie whispered.

'The thing is,' said Johnny, 'all you need to keep warm is circulation. If you were a sailing man, Jim, you'd know that. It's well established that survivors from cold seas are the ones who keep moving about to keep up their body heat. The well wrapped-up ones just freeze. If necessary, drink sea water to vomit; very warmth-inducing.'

'Is that your plan for the afternoon?' I asked.

'He hasn't drunk enough to throw up,' said Bob.

'Would you two please remember that there's a lady present?' said Johnny, and Josie glowed with pleasure. 'In any event,' he continued, 'to prove my point I certainly shan't need any woollen bits and pieces for this afternoon's round.'

'And no kümmel either?' I enquired innocently.

'No kümmel,' Johnny confirmed.

We played off the tenth, I remember, probably because of some important society, such as the flower of St W's playing the Masterful Table of the One-Toed Swamp Sealions. You know the sort of thing, playing foursomes at the speed of Donald Campbell with the wind behind. Anyway, to avoid them we took our position on the tenth and drove off into the light, fresh breeze of a north-easterly. The sun was up and it made a good cocktail with my bracing kümmel. I'm pretty good at steadying the backswing under such conditions, slowing it all down and poking it up, slightly left for choice. Not my natural thing, but pretty necessary on a right-handed dogleg. This I did.

Johnny took the tee. Josie looked quite gormless, staring at him in admiration. Happy visions of his first after-lunch drive presented themselves, but I banished them. I had a nasty feeling that sans-kümmel Johnny might hit a corker. After all, he would suffer neither from over-confidence nor from nagging self-doubt induced by fear of the consequences of over-indulgence.

He did, indeed, hit a corker, and his frizzy little friend let out a gasp of glee, which frankly I found nauseating. Johnny glowed and swelled like a fluorescent toad – or would have done, had his figure not been more like that of a tropical stick insect.

He was a good thirty yards past me, slap-bang in the middle, with a pretty easy approach. If you are well up the fairway on the tenth, the gorse on both sides seems to fall back, leaving a wide choice of seconds between a punched three-quarter five, my own favourite, and a full seven. I, on the other hand, had to give it a full five, and although it was well struck, the slight fade was enough to put it into the edge of the gorse.

Johnny looked positively Byronic in his white shirt and with his black hair, his shirt open and his whole demeanour one of odious romance. Josie gasped as before as he punched another corker into the heart of the green. I chipped rather well, despite the gorse root, and had about a fifteen-footer for my four, but it was not to be.

On the next, having again outdriven me comprehensively, Johnny remarked rather unsportingly, 'Plenty of weight behind the ball, eh?'

Josie looked at me with a smirk, though I don't believe she understood the nuance of what was said.

The round progressed in a pretty unsatisfactory fashion. He played awfully well, which of course I didn't resent, but after every shot Josie let out a little sigh. Then two things happened which, I think, swung things rather my way. First, the sun gradually began to lose its fire, and second, a lucky occurrence really, we ran into probably the only slow foursome ever to play at St Wilfrid's.

'It must be some Americans,' I said. It might seem rather crude racial prejudice on my part, but it was a carefully designed jibe.

'Do you think so? Good God!'

I didn't, actually, particularly since in my experience Americans are far too interested in their own balls to play foursomes, and a fourball has not been played at St Wilfrid's in living memory, at least not in daylight.

'It could easily be, the pace they're playing.'

'What's the point of a Secretary, if he lets any old riff-raff on the course?'

'I don't think you can lump all Americans together that way. They do provide a very good team for the Ryder Cup.'

'I hadn't noticed.'

As you can see, Johnny was in an advanced stage of bravado-itis. I don't really blame him. He was two up at the turn and had just birdied the second, our eleventh. Miss Rafter was gurgling like an infatuated dishwasher, and Johnny cut an impossible figure –

romantic, rubicund and shining with impending triumph of every kind.

It was Johnny's drive on the third. The shadow from the ridge that held the fourth fairway obscured the right-hand rough, and within it were the four, who were rootling around for a ball.

'I'm sure I can play.'

'I don't think so, they're in the rough to the right.'

'They're only Americans. They've probably never heard of waving through.'

Johnny whirled his club in the air like a claymore as he made this ungracious and ignorant remark.

'Maybe, maybe not,' I replied coolly. 'It's a beautiful autumn afternoon, let's enjoy it.'

'Don't be funny, South, this is a game of golf.'

Josie looked at Johnny in some confusion at this remark.

'I thought you enjoyed it, J.D.?'

'What did you call me?'

'J.D., J.D.'

'Don't J.D. me. I'm not a bloody American.'

It was all going extraordinarily well up to this point, so I was irritated to see Josie wheedle up to him, put her tiny hands round his rippling torso and generally make an exhibition of herself.

'You're the best golfer I've ever seen,' she purred in an unappealing manner.

'Be they Yanks, Japanese or Outer Mongolians,

A Green Too Far

they'll certainly complain to the Secretary, seeing you two put on a display like that, and rightly so.'

I really draw the line at people holding hands on the golf course, especially on the tee.

'Oh, do shut up Jim.' He paused and dropped Josie's hand. 'I must be able to drive now.'

'Of course you can. Just shout, "Fore," loudly.'

Well, we got going again eventually, but the tenor of the round had changed. By the seventh the sun had fallen quite away. The foursome in front was moving steadily but no more than that, and Johnny Douglas's gait had decidedly altered: no longer the swagger with his squaw in tow, but more the circular pacing of the caged jaguar. Still a romantic figure, but an increasingly desperate one.

It took me a little while to realise why. It was my need to assume a third jersey that gave me the clue: he was getting very cold.

The final straw came on the ninth, our last. We had been pressing them in a mild kind of way, but they had skedaddled over the hill from the eighth, so when we breasted the hill to stand on the ninth tee there was no sign of them. I suppose that if J.D., as I had taken to calling him, had not been in such a state, jiggling about on the spot like a demented cucumber, he might have looked more carefully. I actually think he was beyond caring. I'm told exposure takes you that way. The wind was now pretty brisk, still from the north-east, so more or less straight into his noble, if frozen, visage, his cheekbones and chin confronting the cutting blow.

'Lovely shot,' I said gallantly.

'Oo-er!' said the girl.

'For God's sake keep moving,' rasped Johnny.

I looked down the fairway with a little more care than he had, although I had a suspicion there might be something to see anyway.

'I think I'll hold on just a moment.'

At that instant the missing foursome reappeared, from bottom left, as it were. I had the distinct impression that one of them turned towards us, as if to give advice, but after a while they played and moved on.

By the time I was able to play, Johnny was sitting in a huddled mass, yearning to be home, I'd say.

Well, we completed the round. I might mention that we'd gone to the ninth all square. I had a four-footer to win, which I took my time over, until with a final, agonised scream Johnny blurted out, 'Have the bloody hole! I can't stand here a moment longer.'

Raging Bull, if somewhat undernourished, had nothing on Johnny Douglas by the time we were back in the clubhouse. He stormed into the members' bar, leaving his friend in the lounge bar, where ladies are invited. To the self-effacing and charming steward he began to let off his frustration.

'My God, Joe, the club seemed to be crawling with

Americans today. And crawling would be a compliment.'

'Really, Mr Douglas? How very unusual.'

'I'm going to have a word with the Secretary. Where the hell is he?'

'Just behind you, Mr Douglas.'

Johnny rounded on the Secretary in time-honoured fashion.

'Seem to be letting in an awful lot of foreigners these days – and slow with it!'

The Secretary fixed him with his small but sharp little eye, burning like a currant in a roly-poly pudding.

'Were you the chap running down the fairways?'

Johnny reddened slightly (probably good for his somewhat inhibited circulation), but before he could answer the stranger behind the Secretary chipped in. He really did have a big girth, and was extremely tall, with whiskers on his cheekbones. 'I've never been called a foreigner before, even coming from the next-door county,' he said.

But Johnny was not to be swayed. 'We were up behind some incredibly slow players. They looked like Americans.'

'Whosoever they were, young man, and however slow their play, it is no excuse to drive through them, as you did on the ninth. There is especially no excuse when you have been running between shots, and when the foursome you choose to drive through includes your Secretary and Captain of a visiting club,' said the Secretary in his most secretarial tone. Suddenly I realised who the big man was, no stranger at all, but the Captain of a most distinguished course further round the coast. As a course it doesn't have the finesse of St Wilfrid's, but it's a bit longer and no one could complain about its use for the Open and that kind of shindig.

'Nice to have visitors from St Crispin's,' I blurted out, in an attempt to inject a bit of bonhomie.

At last the penny dropped with Johnny and he stood there gaping. I think he was genuinely embarrassed. He mumbled some sort of apology and fled for the comforts of the lounge bar.

J.D.'s suffering was, fortunately, not in vain. Not that I'm one to tell people what to eat, but I was encouraged to see as I passed the lounge the warming sight of Johnny sitting beside his frizzy accoutrement. That was not the warming aspect; rather, in front of him stood the largest helping of Dundee cake I have ever laid eyes on, flanked on one side by a jam-and-cream doughnut and on the other by an individual trifle.

I could not resist a friendly nod.

'Got your appetite back, I'm glad to see.'

His eyes seemed curiously glazed and his mouth was too full to reply, but Miss Rafter managed a filthy look and a rather sharp, 'He deserves it.'

'Don't we all?' I countered, and sauntered back to the members' bar. I was beginning to look forward to one of Celia's gourmet dinners.

A Better Mousetrap

Every now and again a new golfing weapon bursts upon an unsuspecting world and the cut and thrust of the noble art is changed, irredeemably.

'No more the mounted Moguls crashing through the rich Roman villas, invincible on their shiny new saddles. Now, the crack of musket destroys the finest of Prince Rupert's cavalry, if you see what I mean. Give or take a few thousand years,' I said with some authority as I leant across the table to help myself to some peanuts.

'You don't mean Prince Rupert; he did rather well. Charge of the Light Brigade, Lord Cardigan and his chaps, more like it.'

Every decent club has a pedant and Alfred Dickins, the distinguished accountant, with his half-moon glasses and all, was ours.

'Well, you see what I mean. Saddle replaced foot, gunpowder defeated horse,' I said, putting it succinctly.

'And I don't believe a Mogul would recognise a saddle if it bit him on the nose,' carried on Alfred, adjusting his half-moons. 'I think you have the medieval knight in mind.'

'Well, that makes an improvement,' said Harry, giving his lop-sided grin.

'Don't worry, Jim, I see what you mean,' said Johnny. 'Scissors beat paper.'

'You mean spoon and fork beats chopsticks,' sniggered Harry. I ignored him.

'No, actually, Johnny, no. I mean,' and I spoke clearly and slowly, 'low-torque Quigley beats wood, steel and graphite.'

We were gathered round the low table by the window in the members' bar at St Wilfrid's, and as the tide withdrew its billows over Ringer Sands and the great red ball disappeared into the Occident, I introduced my fellow members to a new world.

'Have you actually played with a low-torque Quigley?' asked Johnny Douglas.

'Well, no, I haven't actually played with it, but I'm going to, next Thursday.'

Alfred gazed at the peanut dish, his face blank, while Johnny closed his eyes and leant back in the leather armchair. I could see that they were feigning boredom, so I teased it out a little.

'A certain party is coming over from South Africa with a set of clubs fixed with Quigleys. It's pretty hush-hush, of course, because there's some plan to raise a lot of money to develop the new shaft.'

'Easy come, easy go, eh?' said Alfred in a meaning-ful but rather childish way.

'How did you hear about them, anyway? I didn't know you moved in the world of high finance, or at the cutting edge of golf technology, for that matter,' demanded Johnny.

'And who exactly is this "certain party"?' asked Harry. 'Being rather coy, aren't you?'

'Well, they're a pair of world-famous sportsmen, or sportswomen, rather. I think that's all I should say.'

'Ladies, eh!' said Johnny. 'Golfing ladies with a technical bent. Well, well!'

'They can't be that much of a secret if they're raising money,' pointed out Alfred the accountant.

This comment seemed rather sound, so I relented. 'Well, actually they're tennis players, the very best, you know, the Thompson sisters.'

'The Thompsons? Not the doubles pair from the Cape?' asked Harry, positively throbbing with enthusiasm.

Harry had recently been seen slouching round the car park of the town tennis club in forlorn pursuit of a member of the fairer whatnot – or so it was rumoured – a certain Dinah. Given his weight, I don't believe he could serve with any power, let alone produce the running cross-court backhand drive which I'm told is the mark of the true tennis adept. Never saw the point of the game myself, anyway not since I double-faulted with little Sammy (or not so little), events confined to the mists of my early youth. The views on a tennis court are not eye-catching, unlike the view of Sammy, as I seem to remember. She wanted me to choose between her and golf – strange idea, really.

'Yes, the world-famous doubles pair, but all their energies are now plugged into golf,' I rejoined firmly to Harry.

'Dinah said they were coming over to give a demonstration tennis match,' persisted Harry.

'That's not Dinah with the long legs?' asked Johnny.

Harry lost his grin for once.

'Only cover for their gunpowder-packed shafts,' said Alfred.

I detected a note of sarcasm, but you can't expect people to embrace the new without a struggle.

'Very funny. All I can tell you is that my cousin Freddy knows them and assured me that the Quigley could be something big. In fact, he says the flotation of the shares on the stock market is only a matter of time.'

It's surprising how a mood can change, but these few words did the trick. I was quite surprised, really. I never fiddle about with those sorts of things myself, but I sensed I'd roused the sporting instincts of my three fellow Wilfridians; the air had stiffened with their interest.

'Don't lose your shirt, James, old man,' said Alfred, wiping his misted half-moons.

'Those South Africans can be jolly shrewd, even if they're tennis players,' said Johnny.

'Especially if they're lady tennis players,' said Harry.

★

'Cousin Freddy called,' said Celia as I got in that evening.

'Oh, fine. It's probably about Thursday.'

'He didn't say, but he sounded very City.'

'You mean rather pompous.'

'I wouldn't say that, just rather self-important.'

'Same thing. Anyway, if it was about Thursday, he would sound pompous.'

'I'm doing the carrots, dear. Why don't you ring and find out?'

'Good thinking, old thing.'

'Thank you, dear.'

I do like a bit of repartee with my lady wife.

Freddy's son, Fred, answered the phone. His voice was just starting to break, so I thought it was his mother.

'Oh, it's you, Fred. Is Dad there?'

'I'll just get him . . . Pa?' I heard the muffled shout. 'It's Jimbo on the phone.'

'Don't call him that,' I heard in the distance.

'Jimbo,' came Freddy's voice at last. 'You on for Thursday?'

'Of course. I wouldn't miss it for the world.'

'Good show. Any of the boys from the club coming?'

'Can they?'

'The more the merrier.'

'Won't it be rather crowded? How many sets of clubs have you got?'

'Oh, just the set. Didn't I explain? They'll set up in the ballroom at the Lake Park.'

'What on earth are you talking about? I thought we were playing a round.'

'Don't be silly, Jim. You can't test a set of golf clubs like that. It's totally unscientific. No, these are going to be computer-tested. It's the only way.'

So there we were that Thursday evening for the launch of the new shaft, all wired up like some poor mutt on its way to the moon. Alfred, Harry, Johnny and a few others were there, but they were inconspicuous in a room crammed with the eager of the golfing world. The revival of Lake Park was evidence that you can't keep a good course down, nor a bad one.

'Ladies and gentlemen,' said the shorter, elder of the two Thompsons, her hair in two bunches, tied up in blue bows, but her manner 100 per cent business. 'The quality of the new Quigley shaft is going to be tested for you with the aid of the latest in golf technology.'

'What on earth's going on?' Harry whispered to me.

'They've got one of those swing testers. You must have used them.'

'I mustn't have.'

'It uses a photoelectric cell to read the exact position of the club, the angle of its descent and ascent through the swing, its torque, its speed and acceleration at the point of contact. You must know.'

I was able to pass on my new-found knowledge from Freddy to Harry with an authoritative insouciance.

'Do shut up, you two,' said Johnny from just behind us.

'So, ladies and gentlemen, you will see the exact readings on the screen and can make a perfect comparison with alternative shaft configurations,' continued the erstwhile South African tennis heroine.

At length the taller, younger Thompson, a faster serve but slower at the net, took over. Her hair was fair and straight, and from within her tanned features shone out a perfect set of teeth.

'To conduct the test we have with us your own popular professional from Lake Park. Let me hand you over to Arnie.'

After much clapping a man appearing to answer to the sobriquet Arnie stepped forward. Otherwise nondescript, the precision of his coiffure outshone that of the girls. There followed a somewhat tedious commercial for Lake Park and his coaching facilities. Then he said, 'I would be much obliged if I could have three members of the audience.'

Three people at the front rose to their feet, but for some reason this annoyed Harry, who jumped to his feet, crying out, 'Wait on, Arnie, wait on.'

'Yes, sir?'

'Wait on, wait on.'

'Shut up, Harry,' said Johnny with a hiss.

'Let's have a bit of real science, not your three stooges,' barked Harry.

The crowd was somewhat divided at this, some joining Johnny with hisses, others, like Alfred, nodding approval. Arnie, unprepared, was caught off-balance.

'I can assure you the three testers were randomly chosen beforehand,' he said defiantly. His perfect hair-do seemed close to ruffling. 'And they have a good spread of handicaps.'

This united the audience, which gave way to general discourteous laughter. Harry whacked his thigh, as was his custom after sinking a fluky putt. South African ladies are obviously used to this sort of thing, for Thompson taller was quickly up with a sweet smile and cut across the confused Arnie.

'Would the gentleman like to come up and test the club himself?'

This proved a good riposte, because, as now became clear, Harry had made use of the thirst-quenching fac-ilities prior to the exhibition of shaftmanship. With the excitement of the challenge, he leant forward hard on the chair in front to steady himself. The floor, being that of a ballroom, was admirably shiny, the chair unstable and Harry did well not to pitch headlong into the row ahead, chair and all. However, he did enough to amuse the crowd more than a little, and also to disqualify himself as a serious candidate to test the Quigley shaft.

Picking himself off the floor as the laughter died, Harry spoke with unaccustomed dignity. 'I nominate Jim South to test the clubs.'

I suppose that's what friends are for.

It was pretty strange up there in front of the crowd in the Lake Park ballroom, but I did my best, and I must say that according to the computer I did pretty well. The point was that all three of us did much better with Quigleys than with the alternative shaft of a major brand.

'So there you are, ladies and gentlemen, you can see for yourself that the Quigley shaft helps every standard of player. They are, quite literally, the best shafts in the world.'

The applause that followed was really rather nauseating for a commercial display, but I had to agree that the Thompsons had done a good job, with the help of Arnie and Cousin Freddy, his shining dome floating above the crowd, a beacon of intellectual rigour.

'What were they like?' I was asked on all sides as the occasion broke up.

I answered nonchalantly, 'Not bad, really, not bad.'

'Thank you so much Mr South,' said the taller Thompson when Freddy brought her over to be introduced. 'You really saved the day for us.'

'The shafts aren't too bad,' I said warmly. Thompson taller looked a bit taken aback, but her shorter sister bounced in.

'English understatement. I like it.' She laughed and punched me good-naturedly on the shoulder, rather hard, actually. 'Tell you what, you're a good old sport, we'll send you one of the demonstration sets as soon as they're available.'

I accepted graciously.

I must admit I thought no more about it until Celia brought it up over breakfast one morning.

'That new company of Freddy's seems to be doing very nicely.'

'Eh?'

'That golf one.'

'Oh yes?'

'The one you tested at Lake Park. It was all sold out. According to this report, the company's shares have gone through the roof. Did you buy any, dear?'

'Don't be soft, dear, it's all a fix.' I relented a little: 'Though the clubs were jolly good, or at least the computer said they were.'

'I don't understand you, Jim. Everyone at Lake Park bought shares, and Freddy's your own cousin.'

'Exactly.'

'And Johnny Douglas bought a good many, too, or so he said. Even dry old Alfred did.'

'Yes, they do seem to have fallen for it,' I conceded.

It all began to annoy me. After all, how did I know the

computer wasn't fixed? No one had really played with the clubs yet. They might be useless, and then where would all these eager investors be? The whole escapade seemed out of keeping, both with the spirit of golf and with the proper deployment of fiscal resources in a well-founded financial enterprise.

As luck would have it, I had the chance to put all this to Freddy that weekend.

'Oh yes, your Quigleys are in the back of the car,' said Freddy after presenting Celia with some roses, throwing his bags down in our none too spacious hall and relaxing with a cup of tea in the lounge.

'Really?'

'Well, aren't you pleased?'

'Not particularly.'

'Not noted for his gratitude, is he, Celia? Too much living in the land of milk and honey, eh?'

'I think he may be a bit jealous, Freddy.'

'Ah-ha! The little green eye? Dear, oh dear!' Freddy was enjoying this hugely. 'And what has the old sport, as I believe he should now be known, got to be jealous about?'

'Oh, just an opportunity missed. Shares, I believe.'

Freddy positively purred. 'Don't say the silly boy didn't go in for Quigle–Tech? Eh?'

'Do shut up, you two. Of course I didn't. Anyway, I'm sure they're no good.'

Turning to me and looking over the top of the

porcelain teacup, one of Celia's grandmother's, he 'eh'd' me directly. 'No good, eh? And you the tester himself!'

'The truth is, Freddy, they felt extremely odd, stiff-shafted but also whippy at the end. How the computer divined where I hit them I've no idea, but to be honest I don't rate them at all.'

'You are an extraordinary chap, Jim. One minute all on for the new technology, playing an historic role in their birth, the next slamming them off.'

'Well, Freddy,' said I, leaning back in the chintz and exerting the full force of my personality. 'I don't believe a game of golf is ever decided by the clubs. That's all marketing. No, it's skill.'

Celia laughed pleasantly.

'You two! I don't know what gets into you. Come on, Freddy, you've had a long drive, you'd probably like to change.'

After dinner Freddy returned to the matter.

'Do you really believe there's nothing special about the Quigleys, old sport?'

I had had a few glasses by now and was feeling mellow over the thimble of cognac I allow myself. 'Oh, there's plenty special about them. They're specially bad.' A remark I found rather funny.

'Well, if they're so bad, I don't know why you want them.'

'I don't particularly.' Though I was quick to add, 'I

just happen to have been given them.'

'You didn't tell me that, dear,' exclaimed Celia. 'Those Thompson girls are very generous.'

'I'll tell you what,' said Freddy, 'we'll play for them. You haven't still got those old wooden numbers, have you?'

The old wooden numbers, as he referred to them, had been a source of dispute between us for many years. The hickory was rather stiff with age, but I had often pointed out that they played as well with the modern ball as did many a new club. And the spoon, with its single-piece head, could send a ball a solid 200-plus yards, no problem.

'So what?'

'Well, if you've still got them, we can test them too. You always say they're as good as modern clubs. I'll play you level and destroy you and your hickories.'

'You're out of your mind. I might do it for a stroke a hole.'

'You always said the hickories were up there with the best.'

'What do I get when I win? The price of the Quigleys? Anyway, I've only got a mid-iron and a spoon, so I'll have my ordinary sand wedge and my putter.'

'Certainly not, or not for a stroke a hole, anyway.'

'There's no way I'll break a hundred, even with a sand wedge and a putter.'

'What will you do then?'

'A hundred and three, let's say.'

'In that case, with scratch at seventy-one, your handicap is thirty-two. I'm off eighteen, so I'll give you three-quarters of fourteen, that is ten.'

'Ridiculous. Anyway, it has to be full difference now, so that's fourteen.'

'Not if you've got a putter and a wedge.'

We squabbled on for a while, until I came up with the solution.

'We'll play a Sunningdale, two up and give a stroke, okay?'

'Okay.'

'And you want to play for the Quigleys. Fine, but you'll have to give me their value if I win.'

'Okay, but I'll give it to you in shares in Quigle–Tech.'

'If you must.'

So that was settled, and the next day we took to the hallowed turf, a somewhat unbalanced pair. I had a small bag with four motley clubs, while Freddy carried a huge trunk sprouting a full set of Quigleys.

The game, as it happens, was fun. I like wooden clubs, their stiff shafts and light heads, and I played well. The mid-iron blade is rather unforgiving, and I lost two or three holes just from that, but the rest of the game was a pleasant exercise in manufacturing shots. But what made it really fun was the Quigley experience.

Like so many rounds that end in perdition, Freddy's began pretty well, so much so that he was three up in three. He was swinging with confidence, which means slowly, and he was relying on the shafts. I, on the other hand, found it hard to middle the mid-irons and had to concentrate like hell.

'It's three down, old chap. Shall we walk in?' said Freddy in his masterful way.

'Well, at least I get a shot from here on.'

Sunningdale was a good system for that reason, and the fact of the shot began to tell against Freddy. Still, I needed the shots to hang in there, and when we reached the turn I had had a shot on seven holes and was still two down.

'I don't seem to be able to get away from you.'

'Maybe the Quigleys are letting you down.'

'Not at all. If I could sink a putt of more than four feet I'd be at least four up.'

Yes, dear old mother putter. You won't get far without it, Quigley or no Quigley. Anyway, it did its work, the sub-standard putting, and Freddy's swing began to speed up.

'Damn, I seem to have developed a bit of a tendency to hook.'

'It's not you, old man,' I said with a smirk, 'it's Quigle–Tech.'

Freddy glowered and took his stance on the twelfth. He braced, he swung, he attacked the ball with venom. Whoosh! Another hook.

'Damn it!'

I commiserated with enthusiasm.

'I don't know what the matter is.'

I knew; speed, of course. But it seemed a pity not to enjoy the occasion.

'I'm awfully sorry, cousin, but I fear it must be the Quigleys.'

'Do shut up, Jim. I'm wise enough not to blame my tools.'

'But the thing is, Freddy, they shouldn't let you make such a hash of it.'

'No clubs can make up for the really bad shot,' said Freddy.

So it was game, set and match, but I only murmured, 'Oh.'

The rest was inevitable. Freddy got more and more bad-tempered, and naturally enough it wasn't long before his wisdom gave way to rage.

'Do you know, you're quite right, Jim. These damn clubs have a built-in hook.'

'I told you I had no confidence in that computer test,' I said consolingly.

By the end I felt quite sorry for the Quigleys, which were crushed into the ground, hurled into the bag and verbally abused at every turn. The Sunningdale now turned the other way; that is to say, I had to give him a shot on the sixteenth, but I was careful to go to the eighteenth one up, and the £500 slug of shares in Quigle–Tech was mine. It was more than I'd ever dreamed of winning at golf, but it was, after all, only shares.

'You can have them. Now I've played with the damned things I can't get rid of the shares fast enough,' said Freddy with passion.

It was the next weekend at the club that I discovered that Freddy was not the only one disillusioned with the Quigleys. There were some long faces around the bar as I arrived for the monthly medal.

'Fell like a stone on Monday,' said Alfred.

'Didn't touch the sides,' moaned Harry.

'No one had the least idea why, just more sellers than buyers.'

I smiled with quiet satisfaction. I have never approved of easy money. Then I remembered my £500 of shares in Quigle–Tech. It all seemed funny money at the time, but I realised there was probably a lot less of it now.

'I tried to sell mine on Wednesday,' said Johnny Douglas, 'but my broker said there was no bid. Word was they'd been tested over the weekend in some big match and found wanting.'

'The price is still well up on issue,' said Harry.

'Not much use if you can't sell them,' Alfred gloomily pointed out. 'Anyway, if they've been in action, the game's up. Like an oil well, they were much more valuable in undrilled form.'

It rather took the shine off the day and I felt particularly sad for poor Freddy, who had obviously put so much into it. I rang him as soon as I was back home.

'Jim here. Sorry to see Quigle–Tech's in such trouble.'

'Quite so,' said Freddy.

'I hope you haven't come too badly unstuck.'

'Rough with the smooth, old boy, rough with the smooth.'

'Oh, you don't seem too worried, especially after you had such trouble with them last weekend.'

'One has to take a long view, you know.'

'I don't have any interest in that. You couldn't get rid of those shares I won off you, could you?'

'Of course, but you won't get much for them, you know.'

'Well, do your best.'

'Fine, but it won't be until next week.'

'Fine.'

Freddy was as good as his word and he left a message with Celia, which I got on Monday evening.

'Freddy has left some very complicated messages for you, dear.'

'Oh.'

'To begin with, he said he sold your shares for you.'

'Oh, that's good. How much did he get?'

'Not much. A hundred and thirty, he said.'

'That's appalling. They were supposed to be worth five hundred.'

'Yes, he seemed to think you would say something like that, so he told me to say two other things. First, it was a hundred and thirty pounds you didn't have before last weekend. And second, he's bought your shares himself. He said he thought they were good value again.'

'With those rotten shafts?'

'Apparently so. He had one last message: "There's more to life than the bare facts." '

'Well, I don't know what he's on about.' I did, actually. He has something he calls the Greater Fool Theory – you don't have to be brilliant, just less stupid than one other person, and there is always one.

'Well, I certainly don't know – he's your cousin,' said Celia, adding, not very graciously, 'but I still don't know why you didn't buy some shares in the first place.'

'Really, Celia,' I replied, perhaps a little sharply, 'one's got to be true to oneself, in golf and investment.'

She sighed deeply and took a sip of sherry, her eyes fixed on the mantelpiece.

Supper was a little monosyllabic, but I was mag-nanimous enough to say over coffee, 'Anyway, dear, why don't you put the hundred and thirty pounds towards a new potting shed?'

'Oh, James, can I really?' she almost gushed. 'There's a new kind with computer-regulated humidity.'

I winced.

The Root of Success

'Love, money and power, they say, are the mainsprings of motivation,' said Freddy in his usual patronising way.

'What about golf?' I asked.

Celia smirked and started to clear the table.

'Don't you think of anything else?' countered my distinguished cousin. Relieved briefly from the burden of his City duties, he was indulging his penchant for philosophy.

'I thought your theory encompassed all human life.'

'I don't count golf in that.' A low blow, to which I didn't at once respond. 'Anyway, love, money and power, that's all you play for, did you but know it.'

I stood up and followed Celia into the kitchen, carrying a few plates.

'Do go and talk to Freddy,' she said. 'It's his last evening and you know how he likes a good chat. You did beat him both days, you know. He needs cheering up.'

The proposition was fatuous, but I relented none-theless. I returned to the dining-room to catch the end of his peroration.

'So you see, even golf is an expression of the three great forces, if almost wholly diluted by the childish conventions of the ignoble art.'

'Well, I'm off to Hong Kong next week,' I volunteered. 'I'll let you know when I get back from a few rounds what the motivation is over there.'

'You're very simplistic, my dear cousin. Still, enjoy yourself. Whatever else happens, you can be sure they will be unfailingly polite, so don't forget your manners. The true mark of civilisation, old chap.'

He'd obviously borrowed one of Celia's trowels, and was laying it on with same.

'Sounds pretty deadly to me,' I countered in light-hearted vein. 'What do your paragons do for amusement, replace divots?'

'Well, they do play big-money games over there, so take care. And if you get beaten, be grateful it's not with a rattan.'

'That's a thoroughly tasteless remark,' I said.

'I didn't think you would notice. After all, you were well broken in at school.'

This sort of loose comment has always annoyed me. Every age, and every civilisation, has its own punishment system: the cat-o'-nine-tails, the birch, the rattan – no, not much fun, nor meant to be, though whether the sensitive soul finds a hundred hours' community service easier to bear, I know not. Stroke and distance have always seemed cruel enough, not to mention being called to the Secretary's office with the threat of appearing in front of the full committee a short letter away.

'Well, I'm looking forward to it,' I said nonchalantly.

He pontificated, 'I'm told they play skins for large sums. Not long off the tee, but devilish around the greens. By the way, they judge your golf on your luck, not on your skill.'

'Ha!' I cried. 'The fourth motivating force, luck.'

'Don't be a cretin. Luck's not a motivation.'

I had no ready answer, but I had the feeling I'd said something pretty profound.

Skins, eh? I thought to myself as I packed my case for the Orient. You play for a sum on each hole, say ten pence, and if there's no winner, all the bets go onto the next hole. With a fourball you can be playing for quite a sum if there's been no outright winner for, say, four holes. Four times ten pence, times four, plus the stake on the fifth hole. That should be two pounds to win on a golf hole.

I raised the question of luck with Benny Lee as we stood on the first tee of the Old Bridge course in Hong Kong.

'So it's a test of luck, skins, that is, according to my cousin Freddy.'

'I see, Jim, and you don't have luck on your English courses, I suppose.' Benny spoke in clipped tones from beneath his large straw hat with its tartan headband.

'Of course we do, but we think it evens out over a round,' I said.

'How very convenient. You do order things well in the UK.' He pulled down the brim at the front.

'Well, I'm sure it's the same everywhere,' I said gallantly.

'It's never been my experience at Beauchamps. The ball seems to roll into the water wherever I hit it.'

'Oh, are you a member of Beauchamps?'

Just outside London, this was a new course, but already recognised as one of the best in the land, if not yet a great course. It cost a fortune to build and a fortune to be a member.

'Yes, we all are, as a matter of fact.'

Our other two players, Danny Wing and Richard Tan, smiled warmly, if slightly shyly, as they were revealed as tigers of the world-recognised Beauchamps. Danny was tall, but thin and angular, while Richard was on the stubby side.

'We only play in summer,' added Danny, and they all laughed. It occurred to me that the skins game in prospect might be a little competitive.

'Don't worry,' said Richard, as if reading my thoughts from behind his dark glasses, 'Beauchamps likes to have overseas members. We so seldom play.' They all laughed again. Time to concentrate, I thought.

I waggled the end of the club over the ball. The wooden tee had seemed awfully long, but the funny, spongy grass on which we were playing meant that we were all teed up an extra half-inch or so. The tee was damp. The ball was damp. The air was damp. We were all damp. And hot.

Earlier, driving over to the fine Hong Kong course, the air-conditioning going a treat in the pale blue Mercedes, I had gazed fixedly out of the window, not wishing to confront the awful ordeal in store. As a younger man, I had confronted the jeering crowds of fellow salesmen, or anyway a handful of them, but I had conquered that. Here I was, a mature man, or reasonably so, preparing to take on three of the best that the East had to offer, while suffering from jetlag, sleep deprivation and, worst of all, the need to uphold the name of St Wilfrid's in this foreign clime.

Benny had put it well. 'You'll give us all a good lesson, then?'

'Certainly not. I'm sure you'll murder me. Or at least the course will.'

Actually, my spirits had risen briefly when Benny revealed his straw hat, tartan band and all. I had assumed no serious golfer could wear such a thing. Wrongly, as it turned out. How foolish are our prejudices about dress.

'The course is pretty tight, but so short. You'll drive the greens, no problem.'

'I doubt it. What handicap are you off?'

'Oh, we're pleased to get one, and as low as

possible. Not like in England, where you like to keep it up.'

'Well, not really,' I said defensively.

It was an interesting thought, which suggested that Benny had observed the mores of the game closely, and my spirits were beginning to decline again.

'What's the stake?' asked Richard, putting on his dark glasses.

Benny turned to me. 'Twenty dollars okay?'

'Sure,' I replied.

Well, there I stood, my feet sinking into the turf, my head light from the lack of sleep, my limbs heavy from the humid air. I had already said the obligatory, 'Show us the way, Benny, Danny,' and now it was my turn. I took my club back nice and slow.

'Show us the way,' said Benny.

I stopped my swing, lowered the club and looked back at my friendly tormentor. He smiled warmly. I smiled back. Strangely enough, it helped my concentration and I hit a real corker, between the thick tropical leaves and into the bent-grass gully of the third fairway, to the right of the pond.

'Long ball!' said Danny with a whistle, as he peered into the distance like a bird of prey.

I was aware it wasn't straight, and such a remark made at St Wilfrid's would have been clearly sarcastic, but I took it at face value.

'A bit crooked, though,' I said modestly.

'But long,' said Richard, his gravelly voice tinged with awe.

'Yes, well, thanks,' I replied and began to stride off down the fairway, before realising that my three companions were making off towards the electric carts. It did seem a bit feeble to rely on this motorised madness, when the essence of golf is a nice stroll.

'See you at the green,' I shouted to them with some bravado.

My ball had come to rest on some succulent turf just off from the pond. Unfortunately my bag was in the cart, so I had quite a trek to and from it, returning with a seven iron in hand. I took a good solid stance, swished away a bit to give me rhythm and balance and then addressed the ball. Standing there in the humidity, I was conscious that water was beginning to trickle down my back and I was breathing heavily. My head was still quite light, but my limbs were a trifle leaden. Swish, swish. Then, realising that my golf was slow even by the standards of an American fourball, I had a go.

The most destructive thought in a golf swing is the possibility that you are going to have to hit it a bit harder to get it to the green. The heaviness of my limbs, the quagmire in which I was standing and the general sense of uncertainty combined to lead me to heave at it, bringing my shoulders round and failing to clear my hips. I hit the ground behind the ball and splashed it and the deep mud forward about twenty yards.

My next effort was the opposite. The powers of concentration came like ministering angels, and with extraordinary self-control I swung freely. It was a beauty and the ball soared greenwards. I strolled after it, swinging my weapon nonchalantly.

'Nice shot, Jim,' said Benny as I reached the green.

'Which is mine?' I asked, seeing the three balls on the putting surface.

There was an embarrassed silence in which it took me a moment to understand.

Benny found an elegant way of answering me.

'Shall I help you look?'

Politeness had made it difficult for them to point out that I was about twenty yards over the back in a clump of reeds. Anyway, I hacked about a bit while they waited patiently.

'Why don't you putt out?' I called eventually, irritated to be one down so quickly. As it turned out, Richard had a five-footer for the skin but missed it, so the dollars went onto the next hole.

'Don't you find it difficult playing in dark glasses?' I asked Richard, after his missed putt.

'Oh no,' he said, 'it makes no difference,' and laughed deeply.

The next was a par three uphill, and we all cracked

away as before. I played last and hit a pretty good one.

'I'll see you at the top,' said Benny, putting his foot down.

I looked with longing as the little oasis of water, shade and comfort purred up the hill, and I gritted my teeth for the long slog of all of a hundred yards. I could hardly talk when I reached the summit, but I gasped out, 'I think I might take the bus on the next hole.'

'Sure,' said Benny with a smile.

Skins are a funny way of playing golf; rather like the stock market. You don't want to choose the best company, but the company that everyone else will think is the best. So it is with skins. You don't want to play as well as everyone else, you want to play worse or better. Strangely enough, jetlag, sleep deprivation and advanced dehydration make rather a good way of achieving this.

Each hole was one skin, and the winner took a skin. If there was no outright winner, the skin went onto the next hole, until an outright winner emerged who took all the accumulated skins.

'You've got that for it, Benny.'

He was ten feet away and needed that for a birdie. The other two had safe threes, so my three putt didn't worry me.

Benny wrinkled his brow and looked down the line, his putter on one side to make a line to the hole. Time passed. He studied it. The sun came through and I realised he was bound to sink it, as Freddy had explained. However, as the seconds ticked away I became less confident on his behalf and the result was another undecided hole.

'No blood yet,' said Richard with a laugh.

I made hurriedly for the buggy, sank down and drank a pint of water, then another.

I don't know what the statistics show, but with four average golfers on that particular day blood was hard to come by. It wasn't until the seventh that we had a decisive skin.

Richard was playing the best, but he was having trouble with his putting. I thought of mentioning his dark glasses again, but it seemed unnecessary. He had missed from five feet a couple of times, but his swing was beautifully slow and his drives were accurate. Of course if you only hit it 180 yards, you are more likely to be on the fairway than if you hit it 230, as I do, but this may appear to be sour grapes.

'Very steady, Richard,' I said as I made my way to the tee, moving quite slowly, it must be admitted.

'Thank you,' he replied, 'but so short.'

'Not at all.'

Perhaps it did encourage me to show off, and I took a real whack at it.

'Long ball!' sighed the assembled company.

Too long, as it turned out. The hole was a dogleg to

the right, the bright green sward making its way between the purple hibiscus on either side of the fairway, or anyway on the left-hand side, for on the right a fine lake revealed itself as the buggy crested the small rise. Not surprisingly, there was no sign of my ball.

'So sorry, Jim,' said Benny. 'You're in.'

'So I see, or rather I don't.'

I dropped out for a penalty and somewhat desperately took a three wood to the green. It was desperate because to the right was an extensive sandy trough, and to the left a steep hill with more classy blue water at the bottom. For once I managed to hook it.

'More water, I'm afraid,' said Benny in his cheery way.

'Where are you?'

'Just off in two.'

'Congrats.'

'Thanks.'

Silence descended on the buggy, and I used the opportunity to say a few prayers for Richard and Danny. Get lucky, I prayed, which was rather unlikely as Danny, after a good drive, had topped it into the water and Richard had topped three in succession, straight but short.

At that moment the air was disturbed by the sound of birdsong, or rather electronic birdsong, emanating from the side of Benny's bag. He pulled up to a grinding halt on the buggy path and Danny and

Richard did well to avoid us, drawing up alongside.

A fair amount of Cantonese flowed, and eventually Danny and Richard joined in. I deciphered the name of a well-known international stockbroking firm, but otherwise it was incomprehensible, at least to me.

'Anything the matter?' I asked when the conference ended, conscious that spirits were perhaps a little dampened.

'Oh no, nothing, nothing!' they said emphatically.

As it turned out, my three wood was blessed, for although it had rolled down the bank, the thickish grass had held it. I needed a sand wedge to get it clear of the long stuff and overhit it slightly, though in the circumstances of the hole I don't think it was undeserved that it hit a post on the trolley path on the other side of the green and ricocheted back onto the green. I was still fifteen feet away in four, while Benny was just off in two.

Fortune favours the brave, or rather in this case avoids the faint-hearted. Benny fluffed his chip, put his putt six feet past. I sank my putt and he missed his.

Suddenly the oppression of the heat, the humidity, the jetlag, the buzz in my ears, all of it lifted.

They were generous in their praise, despite the loss of many dollars to me, and we purred off to the next hole. Here you played across a lake, which continued up the right-hand side of the fairway. Since the hole ended up a slope, a dogleg to the right, it was quite challenging. No problem if you were long to the left, but a definite mistake to be short to the right.

'Your honour, Jim,' said Richard in a friendly fashion.

'Thanks.'

My confidence had returned and I hit a real beauty, unusually for me with slight draw. Their drives were short to the right. Another skin coming up, I thought.

Danny went into the water, while Richard and Benny both played up level with me. They were getting strokes here, but I reckoned I was well placed.

I was on the downswing of my nine iron to the green when the cheerful chirrup of Benny's phone sang out once more. I flubbed it a few feet.

'Damn!'

'Oh, did the phone put you off?' asked Benny solicitously.

'Well, it did rather.'

'Oh, so sorry. Play it again.'

'No, I couldn't, really.'

'Of course you should, if you're not used to it.'

Richard laughed uproariously at this.

'We'd never finish a round if we played that rule.'

'Why on earth not?'

'The phones on a Hong Kong course, particularly in the afternoon, ring more often than at the office,' Danny pointed out.

I was most confused by all this, but I could see that

my honour was in some way at stake.

'Of course I won't have it again, in that case. Local rules, eh?'

Meanwhile Benny had been spouting away into the phone, and I noticed a satisfied exchange of glances between my hosts when he put the phone down, or rather switched it off.

Jocularly I said, 'I'll be ready when it rings next,' but I didn't elicit a smile.

The net result was that Richard and Benny halved the hole in two fours, and the skins went onto the next hole.

At the halfway stage we stopped and I drank a large bottle of water.

'You want to play the second nine?' Benny asked politely.

He had removed his straw hat and was dabbing his forehead with a wet towel from the drinks carrier.

It was a struggle. I was hot. I was tired. I was ahead. I opened my mouth to say, 'I think I might sit out the second nine,' but the words that came out were as follows. 'Stop halfway? Never heard such nonsense, old chap. Anyway, I've a chance to be the big winner.'

This remark made them laugh a lot, though I couldn't quite see why.

As it happens, I was right to continue. I conserved my energy, shortened my swing and really played rather well. As it happens, so did my opponents. Not consistently, as I was now doing, but often enough to tie up hole after hole. In fact, when we got to the fifteenth all eight skins were riding on it. As luck would have it, I topped my drive about fifty yards, stopping just short of the reeds in front of the lake.

My deadly opponents were not much better and it looked like another no-blood, especially as I'd pulled my seven iron into a mass of thick green leaves topped by yellow weeds to the left of the bunker to the left of the green.

'Damn it,' I said, *sotto voce*.

'Good luck,' said Danny.

'Thanks,' I replied.

'Don't mention it,' said Danny in friendly style.

Damn him, I said to myself as I walked back to the buggy.

'Free drop,' said Benny.

'Where are you?' I asked.

'Not me, you.'

'Me? Why?'

'Local rule.'

'Sounds a good one.' It seemed too good to be true.

'You're in a flower bed.'

'You must be joking,' I said. But Benny, despite his broad smile, was quite serious.

Well, there we were. For some reason the few yellow stems counted as flowers, so I got a free drop, while the luxurious growth of flowering shrubs where

Danny's ball was deposited did not. Lucky, eh?

'Rare species,' said Benny.

I tried to protest.

'You know, at St Wilfrid's we like to play the ball where it lies, whatever the species.'

'Strictly against the rules. Loss of hole,' said Danny.

I shrugged. I looked uncomfortable. I hummed a bit. In fact, I went through the full range of impressions of the reluctant winner. It was quite fun really.

Yes, it was enough for me. I had won the first fifteen skins and the rest was academic. I cruised the remaining holes, confident of victory. I walked out having won fifteen of the skins.

'So you're the big winner,' said Benny with a whistle.

'A cool sixty Hong Kong dollars, eh?' I said with some satisfaction.

'Oh no, Jim. At twenty dollars a skin it works out as a cool seven hundred and twenty. And we always play for US. Not bad for a morning's work.'

The three of them laughed heartily.

Twenty US dollars a skin, I thought. Goodness me, I hadn't been thinking at all. And it could so easily have gone the other way. For the first time that morning I felt cool. In fact, my blood positively ran cold at the thought of how much I could have lost.

Back in the clubhouse I was overcome with euphoria and could enjoy the totality of the experience. The clubhouse was superb. All mod cons, wonderful changing-rooms and a glorious verandah overlooking the eighteenth green, itself almost completely surrounded by clear blue water in which two superb fountains played. You might say it was all a little on the garish side, but I would reply that if you are going to start a new tradition of great courses, you might as well shoot out the lights. They certainly had at the Old Bridge.

'Well, I'm a lucky man,' I said as we downed our Tiger beers and ate some excellent satay.

'Yes, you're a lucky man,' they all agreed, laughing.

'But I hit some pretty good shots, too.'

'Yes, but so lucky,' confirmed Richard.

'Not that lucky,' I countered. I was beginning to feel slightly irritated at this lack of appreciation.

'Very lucky,' said Benny rather sharply.

At this point my cousin's words came back to me, about the Chinese respect for luck.

'Well, I hope that at least I deserved my luck.'

'Like Napoleon's generals, perhaps?' asked Benny.

Was this a joke at my expense? I let it ride.

'I'll tell you what, Benny,' I asked as we made our way back to his car. 'Next time you're in England I must take you to play foursomes at St Wilfrid's. I'd enjoy exposing you three to a windy course with hard fairways and lightning greens. And I've got to give you a chance to get your money back.'

They laughed. 'Don't worry, Jim. The telephone call that interrupted your swing on the eighth was more valuable than a hundred golf games, even at today's reduced stake.'

'What do you normally play for?' I asked, but Benny would only wink at me.

Well, that was the high point of my stay, and I was still glowing from my triumph when Benny drove me to the airport later that week.

'And don't forget, Benny, I shall be mortally offended if you don't come and play at Wilfrid's when you are next over in the UK.'

Benny nodded, a little nervously, I thought.

I did not have to wait long for Benny to come to the UK. We had a pretty good dinner with some mutual acquaintances and over cognac – Benny's, not mine – I drew out of him that he was not leaving until the following afternoon, with nothing planned for the morning.

'You'll just have to play Wilfrid's in the morning, before you leave.'

'Oh, you and Wilfrid's, Jim,' said Benny, laughing.

'You'll love it,' I persisted. 'There's an excellent forecast, fresh and bright.'

'Freezing cold, more like,' said Benny.

'Nonsense,' I countered. 'With plenty of walking and no hold-ups you won't have time to get cold.'

'Not like the Old Bridge, eh?'

This gave me my opening.

'Only one thing. It's too windy for your straw hat, I'm afraid.' Frankly, the thought of Benny wearing the hat at St W's was the only fly in the ointment, and I was glad of the excuse to rule it out.

'I can't play without my hat,' countered Benny.

'I'll be mortally offended if you don't play, Benny. It'll be a day to remember.'

His smile weakened and then evaporated. Lugubriously he replied, 'I'll be honoured to play, if you want me to.'

'See you outside the hotel at seven, then. We'll be down by eight forty-five and teeing off by nine.'

As so often, the forecasters were right about the general blustery weather produced by the end of a depression as it cleared into the North Sea, and it was indeed perfect golf weather, St W's style.

All went as clockwork (digital, I suppose), and my ball perched, ready to be jet-propelled down the beckoning first fairway. And crack it I did.

'Long ball,' whistled Benny.

He took to the tee and waggled the head of the club above the ball.

'Aren't you going to remove your overcoat?'

Benny laughed thinly. 'Maybe in a hole or two.'

'Oh,' I said, beginning to wonder how enthusiastic

Benny really was for the game. He was certainly taking his time, and the awful thought came to me that he might be about to take a practice swing, an almost unpardonable offence at the first tee of St Wilfrid's, made worse because the Secretary was ambling by the putting green, regarding us with the baleful eye of his kind.

'Benny.'

He stopped waggling his club.

'I should have told you, the club doesn't allow practice swings on the first tee.'

He stared at me with blank amazement, wrapped in his overcoat, the wind whipping round his hair, specks of driven rain beginning to fleck his glasses, his mouth gaping at this latest news.

I was about to explain the reason when the trill of a very happy, full-throated bird interrupted our speechless dialogue.

'Good heavens, Benny, that's a very unusual bird.'

He didn't comment but put down his driver and made rapidly for his golf bag, where the bird continued to trill away until Benny removed his cellular telephone.

'Benny here.'

There was a silence, followed by a short burst of Cantonese and then a sign-off.

It had been a short call, but it was long enough to attract the attention of our noble Secretary.

'I'm terribly sorry,' said Benny.

'Don't worry, old chap, I should have warned you.'

'You know perfectly well, South,' began the Secretary.

'It's entirely my fault,' I responded.

'No, it's my fault,' said Benny, 'or at least just a piece of bad luck.'

'Can you make sure it doesn't happen again?' asked the Secretary. 'I must insist.'

'Unfortunately I can't,' said Benny firmly and, turning to me, asked, 'What time can we be back in London by?'

'Well, by eleven,' I answered, somewhat stunned.

'I'm terribly sorry, Jim, but I think we'd better leave.'

The Secretary, who beneath his bossy exterior culti-vated a kindly soul, suddenly looked rather shaken. 'I say, that's not strictly necessary.'

'I'm afraid it is,' said Benny with dignity. 'I'm really very sorry, Jim.'

'I'm awfully sorry about this,' I replied, and even the Secretary joined in.

'I'm most sorry about all this. Please do play on.'

But Benny was adamant, and with the total con-fidence of a small man he put his arm round my shoulder and led me away, his face wreathed in self-mocking smiles.

Our drive back to London was monosyllabic, not on

Benny's part – his face continued to shine like a Dutch madonna – but on mine. I really felt most uncomfortable. Uncomfortable for Benny to be chastised by the Secretary, uncomfortable for the Secretary, who had only been doing his job, and uncomfortable for myself, who had driven Benny all the way to St Wilfrid's, not even to strike one blow at the mocking white pill, and had to drive him back totally, completely, categorically ungolfed.

'So sorry, Jim. No way out, old boy.'

'Well, there we are,' I said as we arrived back at his London hotel. 'Another time, I hope?'

I detected a shadow behind his impassive eyes. He wrapped his coat tighter around him, although we were well within the hotel's stuffy precincts.

'Oh yes, I'd like that.'

And so he collected his key and I bade him a fond farewell. Or almost, for as he walked towards the lift, the receptionist called to Benny in friendly style, 'I hope you got your nine o'clock call on your mobile, Mr Lee, just as you ordered.'

The Secretary Goes Ex

'Words spoken in a moment of passion don't count' may be a good rule for the bedchamber, but it won't make you many friends in the clubhouse. Old Brown, our distinguished Secretary, had never spoken words in a moment of passion, wise or unwise, but it was not his words that were at the root of his eventual exit.

Secretaries, of course, come and go, but the interest lies in the manner of their going. The coming is another matter – a time of quiet optimism, of good fellowship, a new start – and even if the job is hotly contested, the new incumbent is made welcome by all the members.

Not so with the going.

The going never fails to have a tinge of sadness, whether they go from natural causes, jump or are pushed. In a sense old Brown did all three.

'Nobody's perfect,' said Alfred Dickins, displaying his accountant's wisdom as dusk fell and the long summer evening faded into the luminous west.

'And no Secretary can make all the members happy all of the time,' added Bob, tapping his briar into the ashtray.

Harry provided the inevitable tasteless humour, as he slapped his podgy knees.

'Apart from that, Mrs Lincoln, did you enjoy the show?'

'The only person being assassinated round here is old Brown,' said Alfred, getting quite steamed up again and having to remove his half-moons.

'Don't you think it's time we went home?' I said. 'It really doesn't do the club any good to discuss the Secretary, especially one with as many years of exemplary service as Colin Brown.'

I felt the time had come to stand up for a bit of common decency. Anyway, I knew Celia was expecting me back for a late snack and I couldn't face any more attitudinising from the likes of Dickins.

But Alfred wouldn't leave it. 'There you have it,' he harangued us as we rose to our feet. 'Old Brown, for many of us the embodiment of the incomparable spirit of St W's – one false move and the whole golfing establishment of the noble club falls on him like a ton of manure.'

'But he hasn't made a false move,' I pointed out.

'No, he hasn't called into question the paternity of a junior member,' said Harry.

'Nor the sex of the same, despite the absurd long hair you see around these days,' said Johnny Douglas, who had an acute interest in this particular distinction.

'Quite,' said Alfred, still in upbraiding form. 'Nothing at all has actually happened. I mean, if he had confused the accounts in some way to his personal advantage, or had compromised the Lady Captain, say—'

'That would be going it,' interrupted Harry.

'Or,' said Alfred, ignoring Harry, 'say the Captain's Cup had gone missing on the final day. Well, those sort of things would be something.'

This made us laugh and, more to the point, at last led to the break-up of the unseemly gathering.

Over breakfast I tried to explain the situation to Celia.

'The thing is, nobody can quite say what the trouble is. It's just the mood of the club.'

'Well, it seems a pretty bad mood to me.'

'Perhaps it is, perhaps it is.'

'Something must have started it.'

'I suppose so, but God knows what. One Saturday after the last monthly medal someone just started defending Brown, and it was really all downhill from there. No two members were gathered together, but they were leaping to his defence.'

'But for what?'

'If only I knew.'

'There must have been some incident or other,' said Celia with light-hearted persistence.

It was a question I could not answer that morning over breakfast, as the muesli formed a sticky sludge in the bottom of the bowl. Celia surveyed it, and me, with maternal contempt.

★

I took the matter up with the Captain, whom I happened to be partnering in the medal the following Saturday.

'Derek,' I ventured, after I had sunk a long putt on the convex green of the seventh for a birdie. 'Derek, you know the Secretary.' I paused. It was, after all, a rhetorical question, and rhetoric needs time to take effect. 'Old Brown.' I paused again. 'The Secretary, you know?'

Our Captain for the year, Derek Howard, was a big, bluff, red-faced man of great good humour. He had a friendly smile for every member, and would clamp his huge bear-like hand on one's shoulder as he would with his closest friend. In other words, he overdid things a bit; not much, of course, but a bit. I think his election was a reaction to a succession of Captains whose dour demeanours would have put the craggy outcrop of some Scottish hill to shame.

Derek was walking ahead of me, down between the gorse and the thorn to the eighth tee, his large bag slung lightly over his shoulder. He gave no indication that he had heard me.

I persisted. 'Brown, the Secretary, you know.'

We arrived at the tee and the Captain put down his bag.

'Got a two there, eh? Well played.'

It was my honour, so I left the subject of Brown until we were walking down the tenth. I had dropped four shots in two holes, finding the gorse on the eighth and the furthest pot bunker to the right of the ninth to undermine my score. Both errors had been caused by the emergence of a ballooning fade, the classic consequence of undisciplined swinging. I was thus less inclined to be tactful.

'You know, Derek, there's an awful lot of talk going on about the Secretary.'

'Colin Brown? Good old Colin? I don't know where this club would be without him. Anyone says a word against him and they'll have to reckon with me.'

'Oh,' I said, a little surprised by his vehemence.

'I'm sure you're not putting anything out against Colin, are you, Jimbo?'

'Of course not, Derek.' I was quite taken aback by the implication.

'I never thought you would for a moment. It's times like these that the club must hang together, look after its own, form a solid front.'

'Oh, I quite agree.'

'Good show,' he said and hit me rather hard on the back, not exactly helping the preparation for my second. I ballooned it into the gorse beside the tenth, a worse shot even than my fade at the eighth, and for the time being old Brown was sliced from my thoughts.

It was against this confused background that the disappearance of the Captain's prize, moments before it was due to be awarded, made its fateful entrance to the stage of life – or, rather, didn't.

The prizegiving had begun in time-honoured manner. Captain Derek stood there in his moment of triumph.

'It is my great pleasure, as Captain of St Wilfrid's in this memorable year,' and here he cleared his throat and beamed around the room, 'in this memorable year, to present the Captain's Cup to a most worthy winner.'

We had all watched from the clubhouse steps as young Devenish strode up the eighteenth. He looked the proper golfer in his plus-fours and navy jumper, striding along. He was playing Smithson, a nice enough chap in his way but not the sort to set the world alight. Smithson was a little short, so he had to walk rather fast to keep up with Devenish.

Not that Devenish himself was exactly combustible material, but he approached the game with such humility behind his boyish enthusiasm that his some-what pedestrian swing and steady, risk-avoiding tactics were largely overlooked. Smithson, on the other hand, talked a good game but, when it came to it, was no more inclined to take the big risk, like driving for the green on the eleventh, even with the wind behind, than was Devenish.

So when Devenish walked up the eighteenth, dormy, we rose as a man and clapped. Little were we to know that even the great Devenish was capable of nerves. He had pulled into the chasm and was playing his third when he came into view.

'He should still manage a five with no trouble,' said Bob.

Alfred added, 'Smithson won't find it that easy, either. It's clever to approach the eighteenth from the fifteenth green, but only if the wind is from the north-east.'

As it happened, Alfred was wrong, and Smithson was safely on in two. It led, in my view, to old Brown's only false move of the day. He muttered to Smithson as he went by, 'Be turning professional soon, eh?'

'How's that?' snapped Smithson.

'Not out!' said Brown. Though I'm not sure Smithson heard, the rest of us had a good laugh.

Anyway it did no harm to Smithson's concentration, nor to his will to win. He putted up solidly and Devenish conceded. On to the nineteenth.

This was the stuff of legend, or at least would have been. I had often warned the Secretary about the tricky little path from the eighteenth green to the first tee, but to no avail. Devenish proceeded to twist his ankle on that very path as he made his way to the first play-off hole.

So Devenish was carried off, or rather in, somewhat ignominiously, on a trolley reserved for grass cuttings, and the match, nay, the day, the Captain's prize, belonged to Smithson. Thus Smithson had won a technical knockout, as his opponent had retired hurt. Rather an anti-climax, but Captain for the year Derek Howard was going to suck his moment of glory for all its flavour nonetheless.

'So it is a great pleasure, despite the unfortunate accident that befell his worthy opponent, to ask Mr Smithson to come forward to receive the Captain's Cup.' He paused. 'Secretary, could I ask you to bring forward the Cup?'

There was a wait, and a silence.

Harry coughed and whispered to me, 'We usually see the damned thing up there.'

'Secretary, please bring forward the Captain's Cup.' He paused. 'As you know, gentlemen, the Cup is one of the finest trophies of solid golfing silver in this land. Not long ago it was featured in the colour supplement of one of our more enjoyable Sunday papers.'

'The man's rambling,' muttered Harry.

I suppose in every career there comes a moment of truth: the accountant who has added in the date, the solicitor who has conveyed the wrong house, the lion-tamer who has left his head in the lion's mouth, or the golf club Secretary who has mislaid the Captain's Cup.

'Secretary, please bring forward the Captain's Cup,' repeated Captain Derek, adopting a head-magisterial tone, as to a recalcitrant member of the lower fifth.

The Steward coughed quietly, and a way was

cleared for old Brown to step forward with the Captain's Cup. He did not.

It was a whispered snigger from Harry that broke the tension.

'The old bugger's lost it,' he hissed.

It was the sort of remark that threatened to divide the club irrevocably. Half the members were inclined to join in the sniggers; the other half were outraged. For better or worse, our rubicund Captain was in the outraged half.

It was a very awkward situation. Alfred's words came back to me – 'At least he hasn't lost the Captain's Cup,' or something like that – and now the Cup was lost at this critical moment. I tried to catch Alfred's eye but he was staring, his mouth open, as only accountants can.

The Captain grew redder and old Brown was conspicuous by his absence. The situation was explosive.

'Which old bugger?' asked Johnny.

Whether the Captain heard or not, he sensed that he was in danger of losing his audience.

'Where the hell is it?' he sounded off, a volcano exploding in front of the serried ranks of members massed for the high point of the Captain's year.

To this peremptory summons Brown at last responded, at least by presenting his person. Indeed, in the circumstances he behaved with unquestionable dignity. A golf club membership in full cry is not a pretty sight, and the temptation to stand and fight, to decry roundly the absence of the Cup, must have been very strong.

As I say, he behaved with exemplary tact, the perfect tact of the club servant, albeit the most senior one, but a servant nonetheless. He approached with his shoulders back, his head high, his face impassive, almost Nubian in its imperviousness to the drama of the occasion. He leant forward to the Captain's ear and whispered.

There was a momentary hush. All eyes regarded the Captain's already rosy complexion. As he listened, rose turned to red, red to vermilion and, as in some tropical sunset, vermilion to a deep, throbbing purple. Once more the volcano let forth steam, gas and lava.

'What? Mislaid? You mean bloody lost! For God's sake, Brown! Find the bloody thing!' Then, stopping for a moment to tighten the screw another notch, he added, 'Or bloody well get lost yourself!'

The words reverberated round the members' bar. Old Brown stood transfixed. Time stood still. There was a shudder, a judder, an interminable wait, and then with great dignity Brown turned and left the windswept, blasted heath.

I don't expect to become Captain myself – a lot of unnecessary palaver in my opinion – though I suppose that if people insisted I'd give in eventually, but for someone like Howard I can see that this was his moment of triumph destroyed. There's a rather good Americanism about raining on your parade, and there was no doubt at all that a cloudburst of biblical proportions had arrived on Howard's moment in the sun.

The boys in blue, our inestimable guardians of the peace, are no strangers to St W's. I don't mean that we're a hive of the criminal elements, far from it. If some say that in every group of a hundred there is at least one inveterate law-breaker, then I'd say that the members of St W's are the exception that proves the rule. It's rather that the gallant officers of the county swing their woods and irons once a year against the Captain and his men.

So Sergeant Johnson's blue light moved swiftly down the curling camber on the fen road with very little delay. To do Johnson credit, while the rest of us milled around in some disquiet and Captain Howard huffed and puffed to little effect, Johnson moved into the members' bar and thence to the Secretary's office with practised urbanity.

Good fellowship was decidedly sparse and it was Harry who stated the obvious.

'There's no point in hanging around here for a police investigation. Everyone knows Smithson's won. Just say so, and we can all go home.'

'You've got a point, Harry,' I said somewhat disconsolately. I always enjoy a few jars after the Captain's Cup and this was now looking an unlikely prospect.

'Don't talk too loudly,' said Johnny, 'or Captain Howard will tell you to get lost, too.'

This remark cut home with all of us. There was no getting away from it: Captain Howard had put it pretty squarely. The thought of Captain and Secretary currently closeted with Sergeant Johnson, the Captain's words still hanging heavy in the ether, made us shudder.

We finished our bitters – Harry had had another G and T – and we waited. At last Johnson returned.

'Gentlemen, I need detain you no further. I hardly think I need to take statements from you all, but if any member of the club would like to come down to the office in the next day or two we'd be happy to take a statement.'

So the day ended with a whimper, a pathetic ending to a great day, made more so by the sight, in the bar, of Smithson, in an armchair, next to Devenish stretched out on a sofa, drinking alone together, their feats forgotten by all but themselves.

Women are psychic, you know.

'There'll be a perfectly obvious explanation,' said Celia that evening as I told her of the extraordinary events of the day.

'Things will never be the same,' I said, still in shock from the public display of emotion witnessed by one and all.

'Don't be so silly, Jim. You men take yourselves so seriously. Things often go missing and then just turn up.'

'That may be so, but to tell the Secretary to get lost, well, that's another thing.'

'But you all get into such a state! You should forget about it.'

'You don't understand, dear. Alfred actually predicted it would happen.'

'Well, not according to what you said. He just said it hadn't happened to the Secretary up to that point, along with sleeping with the Lady Captain and robbing the members. Have those also happened?'

'Of course not,' I replied with dignity.

'Well, there you are.' Then she added, to my irritation, 'You're behaving like a lot of schoolgirls.'

I wonder why I bother to discuss these sorts of things with Celia at all.

Celia's views would have cut little ice the following weekend in the members' bar, if I had been silly enough to pass them on. The Cup, of course, was rediscovered by Monday, much as Celia predicted.

'You can trust the cleaning lady to be at the root of it,' said Bob between the clenched teeth of the pipe-smoker. In Bob's case his teeth clench even without a pipe.

'Without Mrs Dunstable this club would be a pigsty,' I pointed out. 'And it wasn't her fault someone had left the Cup out on a Sunday night.'

'The Steward must have left it out. He and the Secretary are the only people with the key,' said Bob, aggressive as ever.

'It could have been the Secretary himself, a bit absent-minded, you know,' said Alfred, to whom everyone was a little more absent-minded than he was, and probably intentionally so.

'Well, someone left it out,' said Harry with a laugh, 'and the good Dunstable put it in her pail under a floorcloth in the glory hole, knowing that no one would dare to invade her Empire, and forgot all about it.'

'But why was it left out in the first place?'

'A put-up job by the Steward,' said Bob. 'Brown has been running the place with a rod of iron—'

'A one iron,' interrupted Harry.

'Thank you, Harry. As I was saying,' continued Bob, 'a rod of iron, and our mild-mannered Steward saw his chance to see the back of his tormentor.'

'None of this matters much,' said Johnny, 'but what I can't understand is why old Brown is taking it so badly. After all, as everyone knows, words spoken in a moment of passion don't count.'

'Well, they may not with your little friend Josie or Sheena, or whomever, but they certainly do with old Brown.' I was glad to put Johnny Douglas right and I continued, 'I put the same point to Celia, and she had to agree.'

For some reason they all found this very funny.

So that was the end of the Secretary's reign. We begged him to reconsider. Even Howard apologised in a fairly public way, and the members made their views very clear. Hardly was a hole conceded or a long putt sunk than one member would say to another, 'I do think Brown should change his mind.'

But as the year came to a close, it was clear that Brown was adamant. So St W's set about looking for a new Secretary, and our Captain's moment of passion could not be gainsaid.

'You'll meet the new Secretary when you're next down,' I told Freddy when he called in the New Year.

'Fired Brown at last, did you?'

'Certainly not. It was a very sad affair, but he resigned. A total misunderstanding, you know.'

'I bet you still had to pay him off, a fair whack I should think.'

'We did, as a matter of fact.'

'Thought so,' said Freddy with an unpleasant chuckle, 'I always read Brown as an old shrewdy.'

To Westbourne and Back

We'd all seen the River Ringer roll past the twelfth, even coming up to the tee at high tide, and we were aware that some of our number had a salty past, but it was always a bit of a blow when word went round that a member would not be seen on the links much during the summer because, in the words of the vernacular, he had taken to the briny.

'Married a boat, more like it,' as Johnny Douglas used to say.

It was therefore particularly surprising that Johnny himself should have heard the lure of the mermaids. Admittedly the sun had been benign, the winds south-easterly, force three to four, and the fairways would have put reinforced concrete to shame, but I suspect it had more to do with the burden of his midriff and love not fully requited, a vain effort to recover some purity from the fresh sea spume.

'It's Johnny Douglas for you, dear,' Celia had told me one Tuesday evening at the end of August.

'That's a surprise,' I said. 'He's given up the fairways of St Wilfrid's for the fairways of the ignoble tanker.'

'What nonsense you talk, dear. There's nothing wrong with sailing; my father used to sail.'

107

I was quick to recover my ground.

'Yes, dear. Pass the phone.'

The familiar tones of my former regular partner were quite cool, almost offhand.

'Jim, old chap, I was wondering what you were doing this weekend.'

'Johnny, what a nice surprise. Only last Sunday we were saying that the green swathe would soon be welcoming once more your heavy, or rather steady, tread.'

'No, actually. The thought occurred rather the other way round. How about you giving the old links a miss just one weekend in fifty-two, and letting the call of the sea fill your nostrils?'

'You mean my ears, don't you? Or do you mean the smell of the sea?'

Johnny showed surprising bonhomie.

'Whatever you say, my dear chap. I just thought you'd like a change. After all, you see the curling silver river stretching to the horizon every Saturday; why not follow it, for once?'

The fact is, there lies in the heart of every one of us who has lived in the shadow of this great island's history a special place reserved for the sea; respect, even awe, but also a sense of duty. No one truly of this island can relax happy in the sobriquet 'landlubber'. So, despite my role as leading acolyte at the altar of the mashie-niblick, Johnny Douglas had me on a weak point. It was particularly weak since I had had a lousy month on the rock-hard links, and I had heard that a rest could work wonders, surpassing the magic of the driving range, let alone the untender mercies of the golf pro.

'You want me to abandon St Wilfrid's for a weekend at sea, eh?'

'That's about the size of it.'

'You must be out of your mind.'

'Harry said you got quite vicious last weekend. He thought you might benefit from a change. Anyway, I won't try and persuade you. Give me a ring if you change your mind.'

I returned to the sofa and sank once more into my preferred evening reading, back copies of golfing magazines annotated with my scribbles from earlier ingestions.

Celia interrupted my reverie, or at least my attempt to recover my equilibrium after Johnny's rude importuning.

'What did Johnny want, dear?'

'Some damn fool idea of a day on the sea.'

'Oh, I'd have thought you'd enjoy it.' She looked down at her seed catalogue and added, 'I've always thought you had the makings of a naval man.'

'Don't be ridiculous,' I countered and, picking up my magazines, deposited them under the television and made for bed.

I was quick to slumber, but as I fell beneath the waves of Morpheus, the image of a great three-masted schooner wafting down the River Ringer to adventures I knew not where tugged annoyingly at my trailing consciousness. I could feel the lulling pitch and roll and I drifted off, until I sat up with a start, realising that Celia was climbing aboard. I turned to my ship-mate of many years' standing and, with a steely resolve, said, 'Perhaps I shall take Johnny up on his offer.'

'How nice, dear.'

You could not call *The Lady Ruff* a three-masted schooner, but there was something majestic about making our way seaward down the flooding banks of the Ringer. I was only mildly irritated by the appearance on board of Johnny Douglas's frizzy friend Josie, the secretary at a firm of solicitors who suddenly claimed great familiarity with the ways of the sea.

The tide was flooding at a fine rate as we passed Admiral's Quay and we were high enough to see over the tidal bank to the great course. The low, austere clubhouse topped the dunes, the flag fluttered steadily and the bunkers winked across at us between the blown sand grasses in the early-morning shine that lit up the day.

'Lump in your throat, eh?'

'Yes, there is, rather.'

We were looking across to the fourteenth with its raised green, and I thought of the exquisite roll of the ball from the little dell beyond, from which a well-stroked putt could land dead for an easy three.

'You'll have more than a lump in your throat by the end of the day if the forecast is right,' said Johnny patronisingly.

'What do you mean?' I asked, but he merely laughed.

Laugh he might, I thought, but sea-sickness had never been my problem.

At that moment the boat, which had been making good way into the incoming tide, its sails out to port to catch the steady north-westerly, took a sudden tilt, righting itself and throwing me down into the cockpit.

'Steady, old chap. It always swirls round the harbourmaster's house. Caught you off guard, eh?'

Normally I would have been back at him like a rapier – 'Of course it did, you half-wit, how do you expect me to know what the wind does round the harbourmaster's house?' – but we were at sea, or almost, and although it was not a master–servant relationship, Johnny definitely had the upper hand. It was like being carried in a foursome when your partner is off four and you're off some multiple of that.

Anyway my need to reply was spared by Josie's shriek from below, by which I took some rather unfair compensation.

'No idea about boats, women, but it's pleasant enough to have one along,' Johnny chortled.

'What's the plan for our sail?' I asked when the boat was once more making progress, despite seeming to heel quite hard. Johnny was obviously happy with it all, so I was too.

'There are some maps below which should show you it all. The idea is that we take a steady course south-south-west on this north-westerly until we're off Westbourne, then turn in as the wind backs to south-west, which it should do in late afternoon. The Met. forecast is pretty good, you know: force three, then backing and freshening.'

'Sounds good,' I said, knowing nothing about it.

'It's a fifteen-mile run, and at three or four knots we should take about six hours.' Johnny had a contented smile on his face, his eyes watching ahead for the incoming fishing vessels, his hand steady on the tiller. 'What a beautiful day! I've never been to Westbourne and I'm told the new marina is first-class.'

It was rather a pleasant change to see Johnny enjoying himself without experiencing the usual countervailing irritation that he was playing better golf than me.

'Very relaxing,' I said.

For some reason this seemed to annoy him and he countered, 'Wait and see.'

'Why doesn't Josie come up here?'

'Oh, I think she's happier below,' he said with a twinkle in his eye.

We were just turning into the sea at the mouth of the Ringer. I took one last look at St Wilfrid's disappearing beneath the dunes and thought to myself that Celia was right. It does an Englishman good to fill his lungs on the high seas once in a while.

We had left harbour at noon, planning to reach Westbourne at 6 p.m., so at 2 p.m. I went below to look at the charts. From what I could see, Mallory Cliffs were still west of us, even though we were quite far out. Josie was asleep and I tried not to wake her. She was snoring gently.

Back in the cockpit I asked Johnny, 'How are we getting on?'

'Not bad.'

'Seems to be a bit more wind, anyway.'

'Yes.'

'Tea in Westbourne, eh?'

Douglas didn't reply but kept his eye on the oncoming waves. They were now lifting and dropping us with a fairly sharp bump as the nose of the boat made headway into the spray, which occasionally splooshed over the front of the boat.

'Ah, this is the life,' I volunteered as another bathful of spray hit me round the side of the head.

Johnny smiled thinly. 'You'd better close up the cabin roof completely,' he said.

At that moment a rather tousled-looking Josie appeared.

'What's going on?'

'Nothing much,' said Johnny.

'It seems awfully rough,' she whined.

I looked at Johnny for his reply, expecting a condescending smile.

'Not particularly,' he replied rather blankly.

'Let's go back, Johnny. It's horrible.'

This really shocked me. I had at least thought Josie would be a sailor.

A sheet of spray crossed the front of the boat and reached Josie's neck. She let out a rather unladylike expletive, which I must say by this time did not surprise me, and went below.

'No determination, women,' I said.

'No,' said Johnny.

At this moment I thought of Celia and wondered how accurate my earlier prognostications had been.

Johnny was certainly showing a bit of determination, which rather surprised me. You see, I knew Johnny Douglas pretty well, and I could tell the difference between an evening stroll around nine holes, the sort of sail that I presumed we were on, and the Captain's Cup – I mean at St Wilfrid's, not some blasted thing round the Isle of Wight. From the furrow on the old hacker's brow it was clear that our sail was a bit more than a stroll.

'You don't think we should go back?'

He turned his face from the oncoming waves for the first time in a while.

'Listen, Jim, when you're on the fifteenth and you get a few drops of rain, do you walk in? No, of course not. Well, we're at sea, and you can walk in if you like, but that's your affair.'

Huh, I thought. It all reminds me of Johnny three putting in the Bloxall Challenge Cup and blaming everyone else.

'Okay, Johnny, I was just asking.'

'Anyway,' he added after a particularly heavy wave, 'we can't get into St Wilfrid's until the next high tide, so Westbourne's our best option.'

'What else could we do?' I asked innocently, but the noise of the wind in the rigging obscured his reply. 'This wind must be helping us along.'

'It's backed a little sooner than I'd hoped,' he revealed amidst the spray. 'We're going to be straight into it all the way to Westbourne.'

Well, we didn't talk much after that. I sat perched up on the side of the boat, watching the variety of green surges coming towards us, most with white spray tops, and calculated how much spray each would give us, trying to duck my head accordingly. Little streams of cooling sea water ran down my back. After a while I began to imagine hitting golf shots over the incoming waves, and this turned into a subliminal wish to be back at St Wilfrid's. I even began to ask myself why I was on this boat at all. But I caught myself in time, cast away the gloomy thoughts, threw back my shoulders and said to myself: Am I disheartened? Hell, no! At this moment another bucketful descended on my head and I licked the thick salt off my lips.

Time passed – bang, sploosh, whoosh; bang, sploosh, whoosh – until the cramp in my right leg stirred me to action.

'We don't seem to be making much progress.'

'We're going fine.'

'I'll look at the chart.'

Maybe this was a good move, maybe not. On careful study below, avoiding Josie, who lay on her side facing the wall, I deciphered what I had long suspected. The seaside resort of Peastings, whose pier we were just passing, did not represent the last stop before Westbourne but barely the halfway stage.

Coming up, I passed this news to Johnny.

'I would say on the map we've still got ten miles to go.' I added with a little acerbity, 'What time do you make it?'

For the first time I saw on Johnny's brown orb the wash of pallor.

'Are you sure?'

'Of course I'm sure. Anyway, I thought you knew the coast here.'

He set his jaw and, with the bravado of the poor

sport who has left his partner fifty yards short at the third, remarked coolly, 'Of course, I knew that.' He might have added: Anyway, you chip better than you putt.

So we bashed on, slowly leaving the pier behind, as the sun began to make its steady descent in the sky. At six-thirty, almost exactly, Johnny jumped into action.

'Well, that's been most amusing. I think we'll go back now.'

'Go back?' I shouted. 'But you said we were making such good progress!'

'I'd always planned to turn about here. We should be back at Wilfrid's in time for a nightcap.'

'A nightcap? But it's only six-thirty!'

'Well, we can open the *vino*. The thing is, we won't be able to get up the river until two hours before high tide, and that's tennish.'

And with that he turned the boat and a curious lull descended, interrupted only by the fizzing of the water as we creamed down the waves with the wind behind us.

'You take the tiller, old man. Just don't let it gybe.'

'Don't let it what?'

'Gybe! Don't let the boom come across.'

'Why not?' But he had left to go below.

Shortly afterwards the wave coming up behind got a little kick in it, some rebound from the shore, I suppose, and the boat frisked to the side. There was a terrific crack and, when I opened my eyes, we were running in to shore, with the boom on the other side.

It was really rather impressive, the speed with which the boom had come across, but rather more impressive was the speed with which Johnny, hurling himself out of the hatch to the back of the boat, grabbed the tiller and took us out from the fast-approaching shore.

Again there was a lurch of monumental proportions, but this time the sail had been hauled in, so the big, whacking boom moved across with a reasonably controlled lurch.

'I suppose we gybed. Sorry about that,' I said with a degree of contrition. After all, I had received an order and I had not obeyed it.

Johnny was excessively alert, looking fore and aft, as they say, with great urgency.

'Don't worry, old chap. It was just as well you had your head down.'

He was really quite nice about it.

Then we saw a water-ski boat come looping out from the old pier, jumping the waves in plumes of spray. Pretty impressive, it looked. Wouldn't mind being on that, I thought but didn't say so.

They roared around a few times and seemed to be heading back when Johnny waved at them. They came alongside, as far as they were able to in the lurching sea, and he shouted at them, 'You couldn't do me a favour?'

'How's that?' shouted back the rubber-clad driver. The stubble on his head was quite a bit shorter than that on his chin, and gold rings dangled from his nose and ear.

'We were going to Westbourne, but the seas are too heavy, so we're going back to Wilfrid's. Could you tell the harbourmaster at Wilfrid's?' shouted Johnny as we swayed up and away from the roar of the speedboat.

'Heavy going, eh?' laughed the piratical driver and, turning to his long-haired co-driver, said, 'Get the club on the blower.'

While the crackling VHF did its stuff, I examined the large outboard on the back.

'Forty horsepower, squire,' volunteered the driver.

It did have its appeal but it was somewhat hard to appreciate on the tossing briny, and even harder to imagine that in a few short moments our new friends would be back ashore, while we would continue on our lonely journey back to the ancient town of St Wilfrid's.

'You couldn't give my wife a ring while you're about it, could you?' I asked when the message had been passed to shore.

'And why not?' asked the long-haired one. 'I'll even give her a visit, if you like.'

The mind boggled, but I laughed politely and shouted out the number, adding, 'If you could just say we'll ring from Wilfrid's.'

'No probs.' And they revved their engine, about to

tear off into the salty cascades.

At that moment Josie appeared. Her hair was in a scarf, her jacket nicely buttoned and even her lipstick seemed in place. In her hand she held her small overnight bag. We all looked at each other but the message was clear.

Not a word was spoken as I reviewed the resignation on Johnny's face, a sly smile on the face of the speedboat driver and steely determination behind Josie's eyes. Dropping the pilot? The rat leaving the sinking ship? The last moments of the *Titanic*? No, it was a clear case of declaring the ball lost and conceding the match. I found the image calming, particularly Johnny's helpless grimace, which brought back many a happy memory.

The lost ball safely embedded in the back of the speedboat, so to speak, they turned their nose and tore off in a cloud of spume, while we rolled off along our drunken path.

'I'll get the mainsail down and then we can open the claret, now there's fewer mouths to fill,' said Johnny in sudden good spirits.

It was really very pleasant after that. We had about a five-mile run, and with the sun setting and the tide not up at our mooring, there was no hurry. Indeed, the night was well set and the lights sparkling along the distant roads by the time we nosed towards port, two bottles of claret and a lot of fruit cake later. The wind was dying and we slopped along on the remains of the rollers, our jib valiantly pulling us towards our goal, as through my somewhat incoherent brain ran the words of the poet Tennyson, 'And the sun went down, and the stars came out far over the summer sea,/But never a moment ceased the fight of the one and the fifty-three'. It seemed appropriate at the time, search me why.

My reverie was broken by car headlights on the sandbanks that guarded the noble links.

'Must be the urge of young love, testing the sea defences,' remarked Johnny in his single-minded way.

'More like OAPs, in this part of the world. Some old chap who can't sleep, I expect,' I countered.

'You underestimate the primeval urges, shipmate.'

'I know,' I said with real enthusiasm, 'it's probably Josie and her new friend with the gold rings.'

'Do shut up.'

We were gliding in gracefully.

Suddenly the sea lit up as a searchlight picked us out. I looked at Johnny and was glad to see that he too looked startled, positively rabbit-like, actually. Then a voice broke the cries of the seagulls.

'Is that *Lady Ruff*?' it boomed out.

'What?' shouted Johnny.

'Is that *Lady Ruff*?' it boomed again.

'Not any more,' I shouted. 'She's gone ashore.'

'Shut up,' hissed Johnny. 'Yes,' he hollered. 'This is *The Lady Ruff.*'

'Is that *Lady Ruff*?' it boomed again.

'You're wasting your breath,' I said to Johnny.

'Yes, I suppose so. We'll just sail in.'

The large light made it difficult to see the steep sides of the river bank but at last we made it, and out of the wind we were finally able to converse.

'Is that *Lady Ruff*?' came over the Tannoy.

'You bet,' I called.

'She suits me,' shouted Johnny.

'Are you in need of further assistance?' came the disembodied voice.

'We haven't had any yet,' shouted Johnny.

'Unless you count the Ruff stuff,' I chipped in.

'Where is your mooring?'

'Dune Quay,' shouted Johnny.

This seemed to satisfy the busybodies, for the light steamed off into the night.

We moseyed down the flooding river, calm after the storm, the night well in place and a slight ache of tiredness beginning to suffuse my no longer hearty bones.

'Go up front and test the water, shipmate.'

I had grown used to Johnny's patronising carry-on, but this was ridiculous.

'Not at this time of night,' I replied curtly.

'I mean the depth, you bonehead.'

I went dutifully aforeships, as they say, and peered into the murky depths.

'I can't tell.'

'Wait till we're up to the moorings and then tell me.'

I saw what he meant, for by the light of the strong torch I realised that the tide barely covered the mud-banks on which *The Lady Ruff* customarily rested her stately rump.

'Shallow water,' I cried out.

'Are you sure?'

'Yes!'

'Oh, well.'

Ignoring my advice, he took her straight in and to my surprise we splooshed gently up to our mooring. A large figure bent down and proffered a huge hand, or so it appeared in the pinpoint light of the torch.

'Mr Douglas.'

'No,' I said quickly, refusing the large mitt.

'Is he aboard?' asked the mitt.

'I'm here.'

'Mr Douglas?'

'That's me.'

'We've been looking for you for four hours, Mr Douglas. Don't you have navigation lights?'

'Well, now you've found me, how may I help?'

'We understand you were in difficulties.'

'Well, you understand wrong.' He paused. 'Although we're obviously grateful for your interest, you can rest assured we've been having a very pleasant sail.'

'What about your navigation lights?'

'We're under seven metres, so we don't need more than a white light on the masthead.'

'But you didn't show any lights.'

'There was no point. We were the only people at sea. Anyway it would have made it difficult to see.'

'But it would've made it easier to be seen.'

'What would've been the point of that? After all, no one wanted to see us.'

'Well, we did.'

'That was your problem.'

I listened in wonderment to this conversation. Playing through a slow fourball, not that such a thing could exist at St Wilfrid's, was nothing compared to the erudition of these men in the art of repartee.

'Have you flares aboard?'

'Lots.'

'Are they in date?'

'Some of them.'

And so it went on, quite amicably, really, until the final question.

'A last question, Mr Douglas. Why didn't you contact us on your VHF?'

'Because my VHF doesn't exist. I can't see the point of them.'

This, as it turned out, was game, set and match to both sides.

The stunned silence was followed by gales of true hilarity. Johnny had hit the funny bone, the unanswerable proposition, a sailor who saw no point in VHF. Conversation was clearly not worth pursuing and, with a final gust of mirth, the mitt shook both our hands and, perhaps fearing for his own sanity, left us to the dank and very dark mooring of our berth.

We tied up as best we could and crawled into Johnny's car.

I did my best not to make too much noise as I said goodbye beneath Celia's window half an hour later.

'Thank you, Johnny, for an extraordinary day.'

'Quite a change from the green swathe and the little white ball, eh?'

'There's really no comparison. You don't seem able to win at sailing.'

'Don't be so small-minded, Jim. You're up against the elements in all their glory.'

'You seemed to be up against the harbourmaster.'

'You must admit, it was pretty exciting with those large rollers, and that moment when we gybed. You must have been pretty shaken up.'

'What?' I asked, trying to get the hang of it all. 'Were those waves large? And the gybe? Was that a real problem?'

'Well, it wasn't ideal, I must admit. In fact, it wasn't

great when we almost broached. We could easily have rolled.'

'Wait a minute.' I was getting quite angry. 'Do you mean our sail was not the usual thing?'

'Let's just say it wasn't that unusual.'

'Let me put it another way, Johnny. What would be your sailing handicap?'

'Oh, I don't know. They don't trifle with that sort of thing on the high seas.'

'Well, I think it's time they did, because I don't think you'd make it through the first round.' I said this with real force.

'You may be right, old shipmate, but you must admit it's been quite an adventure.'

He was, of course, right, and in my heart I was rather pleased that it had been a bit ferocious. Perhaps I was lucky I hadn't known all this at the time. But it still irked me that Johnny Douglas's clear defeat at the hands of Neptune should not produce more tangible evidence.

I reckoned Neptune had won seven and six, but no dog-licence had been issued. Still, I fell easily into a deep sleep as my head hit the pillow – no chips fluffed or short putts hooked to disturb my dreams.

Single-minded

We saw the figure as we breasted the dune ridge that divides the thirteenth, a great hole requiring a blind brassy, as they used to say, normally into a stiff sou' wester.

'Where did he appear from?' asked Cousin Freddy, his massive cranium shining in the spring morning, his few remaining hairs ruffled by a slight, if chill, wind.

'No idea,' said I.

'Must have cut across from the clubhouse.'

'I'm sure I cleared the long stuff.'

'He must be a single.'

'I didn't think the wind was that strong.'

'He's probably playing the eighth and caught a flyer past the bushes behind the fourteenth.'

'I hit it pretty well.'

'It's always an odd sight, a single. A special sort of dedication, a self-obsession without the possibility of relief by a partner,' mused Freddy.

'You must have seen it. You were on the top of the hill,' I said with perhaps a touch of acid in my voice.

'What? Haven't you found your ball yet?'

'No, that's why I'm still looking. Want to give me a hand?'

'Oh, sorry, old chap. You're just down there beyond the bush.'

'Why didn't you say so?'

'Where would you be without your partner, eh?'

I hacked out, playing a low runner to the undulating green, but missed the putt to lose the hole.

'All square,' said Freddy as we left the green.

I humphed. It was annoying really, particularly since Freddy had fluked a long putt on the previous hole.

Beside the fourteenth tee, to tell following golfers that the green was clear, stood an old bell.

'Sound the Lutine,' I commanded, clean forgetting that Freddy was a Name at Lloyds.

He winced.

'Oh, sorry, I forgot.'

'Don't worry, old chap.'

'It must be an awful worry.'

'Well, it was, but I've doubled up. Anyway, let's play this excellent game.'

'Good idea.'

'Hold on, that chap is still up there,' said Freddy, noticing the lone golfer still rootling around on the fourteenth.

'Just shout, "Fore," ' I advised him. He's got no standing.'

'Don't be so aggressive, Jim. The poor chap is suffering on his own.'

'Well, I'm suffering with you. That's probably worse.'

He stared into the sharp breeze.

'Do get on with it,' I said.

At last Freddy took his stance on the tee and wielded his four iron. His timing was perfect, for as he came down from the rather over-arched pivot at the top, the single looked round and waved.

I'm probably flattering Freddy's golf to describe it as a swing – it's more like a controlled lurch with menace, followed by an ugly flick – but it had enough rhythm for the wave of the lonesome to disturb the finely balanced mechanism. Freddy's right hand came round with too much flick and the ball raced up and to the left, into the hill above the hole. I could visualise it bouncing down into one of the shrewdly placed pot bunkers.

'Blast!'

'Hard luck.'

'He waved just as I played.'

'Oh, did it put you off?'

'Humph.'

'You may have ended quite well. Anyway, I told you to shout, "Fore".'

'He wasn't on the green.'

'Exactly,' I said and laughed in a good-humoured way.

Freddy shot me a pained glance, but he knew quite well that he hadn't hit the fourteenth in all the many years he had been visiting me and mine at St W's sur-la-plage.

I hit a good solid ball, perhaps a little short but running onto the apron, leaving me with a long but relatively flat putt.

'Found yours?' I asked.

'It's just up above the middle bunker,' said a somewhat reedy voice close by the thorns that separate the eighth from the fourteenth. It was the Lone Ranger, still waiting. He added helpfully, 'You're caught up in the Fieldmouse-Ear. A bit lucky, really.'

'Do you hear that, Freddy?' I shouted above the wind. 'You were lucky, you're in the Mouse-Ear.'

'No, no, the Fieldmouse-Ear.'

'I've never seen a fieldmouse round here,' I said, turning on the lonely fellow. I was beginning to see why he was alone.

'You call this lucky?' broke in Freddy. 'I've got to chip out of this rubbish over the bunker onto that pig of a green. What's lucky about it, Jim?'

'I didn't say it was lucky, our friend did.'

'It's not rubbish, it's really quite rare,' broke in our new friend, his brown pointed nose stretching out from his small moustache under his tweed cap.

'You mean the Fieldmouse-Ear is quite a rare plant?' I asked.

'Yes, in places, and it's nice to see it here in abundance.'

'Oh, I quite agree,' I said.

'Stand clear and shut up, Jim,' said Freddy.

Single-minded

Freddy was right; it was a difficult shot. His ball flew out, landed on the middle of the green and, spinless, scooted off into the long grass below the sleepers to the right of the undulating table, shining beautifully on that glorious late spring morning. He was still further away than me, having reached the long grass.

With a face of thunderous intent Freddy strode across the green, making for the general area of the ball.

'You'll find it next to the clump of Ragged Robin,' called out the single.

'The what?' spluttered Freddy.

'The Ragged Robin.'

'Speak English, man.'

'Those straggly red flowers with narrow leaves.'

'Pretty rare, too, eh?' I asked innocently.

'They're quite well known, you know,' our friend said, turning to me.

'I don't know,' said Freddy with increasing venom. 'Please simply point out the ball, omitting the botany.'

'I thought all golfers knew their wild flowers,' he said in genuine surprise.

'I thought all golfers knew better than to wave in the middle of a shot.'

At this the Lone Ranger looked suddenly embarrassed and asked my favourite question, with apparent sincerity.

'I didn't put you off, did I?'

Freddy was in a cleft stick with this one. Admit that he was put off and appear a feckless, nervy golfer; say that he wasn't, and obviously lie. And the beauty of it is that, once put off, it's a long road back to the steadiness of purpose and faultless equanimity that makes the winning golfer. His only hope would be to put me off, and my mood was much too good for that.

Walking up to the fourteenth tee, Freddy was about to start but I forestalled him.

'Well, that was very hard luck. One down, I think.'

'I don't know what the man is doing on the course. Some damned new member, I suppose. He seems more interested in flowers than golf.' This was followed by the inevitable, 'I don't know what the club's coming to.'

Music to my ears. What's the club coming to, what the club's coming to, what *is* the club coming to, all delightful preludes to decline, demoralisation and defeat.

He plonked his second in the bunker at the end of the valley at the fifteenth, wriggled briefly with a good splash out, but took three from the edge to be fairly gaffed. On the sixteenth he hooked it duck-wise, a real creamer, over the twelfth green into the heavy long stuff. He repeated the performance with his provisional, threw his club to the ground, picked it up and said, 'Thank you for the match, Jim. It suits me, really. I want to be up in London by early afternoon.'

'Suits me, too,' I said smugly. 'And be careful you don't tread on any Fieldmouse-Ear on your way back to the clubhouse.'

I felt quite well disposed towards the Lone Ranger in consequence of it all, and fell into conversation with him once back in the clubhouse, Freddy safely en route to Londres. We sat supping some very passable ale, which the new Secretary had somehow inveigled the old Steward to introduce.

'You seem to know an awful lot about flowers. For a golfer, that is.'

'Oh, do you think so?'

Our man seemed somewhat surprised, but on the whole flattered at the suggestion.

'I'd say. I doubt if there's more than half a dozen members who know their Sheep's Foot from their Lady's Ear,' I replied with some enthusiasm.

'Sorry, I'm not with you.'

'Well, you know, their Elephant's Buttercup from their Vole's Nose, or their Bat's Hat from their Purple Grass.'

'Oh, I see what you mean. You're making them up. Yes, well, I do know a little of England's wild flowers.'

I didn't pick up the nuance there, so I pressed on.

'But don't you find it boring playing on your own?'

'Oh, not at all. I find it more relaxing, less demanding, and quite truthfully less stressful.'

'Yes, but there's no one there to admire your good shots.'

'Oh, is that what you do?'

'Well, perhaps not exactly.'

'When I hit a good shot it doesn't seem to please my opponents, even if they mumble some muted praise.'

'Oh, I don't know. I think golfers are pretty generous, in the main,' I said with as much conviction as I could muster.

We supped our ale and I watched with friendly amusement as a thin line of foam attached itself to his small moustache. It was altogether straggly in appearance, not unlike the unprepossessing wild flower he had remarked upon. I studied him as I imagined he might study a wild flower. He had pepper-and-salt hair just touching his slightly frayed collar, repeated in diminutive fashion out of his nose and ears. The whole might have struck one as somewhat rat-like, had it not been for his large brown eyes.

'I suppose, playing on your own, you get lots of chances to follow the flora.'

'Well, yes, I suppose that's true,' he said with considerable embarrassment. 'The way I play I get lots of chances to study the more distant sierras of St Wilfrid's.'

'Well, I think it's a fine hobby. We're lucky to have you in the club.'

I wanted to boost him a bit. I sensed his morale

was a little low; perhaps he was lacking innate self-confidence.

I continued warmly, 'You ought to get the Secretary involved, give him something to do,' by which I meant it would keep him out of trouble, but I felt it might be a little indiscreet to be too explicit with this chap, whom I didn't really have much of a lead on.

'Do you really think the Secretary would be interested?' he asked doubtfully.

'I don't see why not. He's new, too, you know.'

New members do have an awfully difficult time. My friend seemed pretty nervous of the whole idea, so I called over irascible Bob, who I'm glad to say had just extinguished his rank-smelling briar.

'Our friend here is an expert botanist, you know.'

'You don't say,' said Bob warily.

'Come on, Bob, he's a new member. Let me introduce you.'

I turned to my new friend at this point, expecting him to introduce himself, but he didn't pick up the clue, so I pressed on.

'This is Bob Ashworth, and you are?' I let it hang in the air with a question mark.

'Oh, I'm David Fairbeat. But I should explain—'

'How do you do, Fairbeat.' Bob was in pompous mood, the kind especially reserved for new arrivals.

'Oh, how do you do.'

'Call him Bob, Dave,' I instructed, and to raise the

general level of bonhomie I added, 'Dave knows more about wild flowers than you do about the gorse to the right of the tenth.'

'Damned nuisance, just another place to lose your ball.'

I suppose people get away to their club at the week-end to relax, which for many of us means saying what we feel, but I was a little disappointed by Bob's approach, something I made quite clear with my following remark.

'*Chacun à son goût*,' I said, 'but the plan is for Dave to make a full inventory of the wild flowers of St W's. In fact, we're just about to broach the whole matter with the Secretary.'

'You'll get his support, all right. Anything new will go down well with him – positively African.'

'Do you think so?' asked the putative botanist, obviously confused by the general line of Bob's remarks.

'I'm afraid so. Nothing he'd like more than to cordon off whole areas of the course because some rare weed has been found.'

'Steady on, Bob,' I said, though I must say the thought had not occurred to me until then. It was not encouraging. 'That couldn't happen here.'

'Don't bank on it.'

'Did you lose badly this morning?' I asked him.

It was the least I could do to try and level things up, and I was rewarded by a scowl and some prodding of the briar. At that moment the Secretary appeared and all was explained by his clap on Bob's shoulder and his witty remark.

'Don't take it so hard, Bob. Somebody has to lose.'

To Bob's credit he managed a thin smile, perhaps considering he had had his justified sulk, and showed the natural good manners of our fellow members.

'We've a proposition here,' said I. 'Our newest member is reputed to be a world-renowned botanist and would like the club's support for a study of St W's flora. Good idea, eh?'

'Good idea, good idea! It'll put us in great shape with the Greens. Good idea!' the Secretary blurted out.

'Oh no, not the greens, anything but the greens,' counter-blurted Bob.

'Which greens?' I asked, confused.

'The political ones, not the round ones.' The Secretary laughed.

'I can't think those Greens could care less. It isn't as if we use much fertiliser round here, not like some of those inland courses,' I said, finally catching the point.

'Perhaps so,' said the Secretary with a note of disappointment, 'though that sort of publicity does the club no harm.'

'And no good,' added Bob.

'A green too far,' butted in Harry with a silly laugh.

'I think I should explain,' said the new member.

'Yes?' said Bob.

'Well, I'm not really a new member.'

'What are you, then?'

The Secretary came to his aid.

'Oh, it's Mr Fairbeat. Of course, I should have remembered.' Turning to Bob, he said, 'Reciprocal arrangements with the Argies, you know. One of my little introductions. And Fairbeat here is our first and, as you can see, as much one of us as the next one.'

'Quite so,' I said loyally.

'I was brought up in England, as a matter of fact, but I've been living in Buenos Aires for twenty-five years now. I'm a member of La Corsa Grande, you know,' explained David.

'A bit like coals to Newcastle,' said Bob.

'Well, what could be better than to use his expert skills to our advantage,' I continued. It is often better to ignore the tactless remark.

'Now I'm afraid I must be off,' said the reciprocal member, rising rather abruptly.

I rose, too.

'A pleasure to see you, old chap. I hope we'll see more of you.'

'And I look forward to seeing your inventory of the flora,' added the Secretary to David's retreating back.

I didn't see anything more of David Fairbeat for a week or two. The next time was when I was playing a

foursome with a few of the regulars, and I caught sight
of the tall, reedy figure in some deep grass in the
chasm to the left of the fourth. We were playing the
seventh, and Alfred had stubbed the ball into a piece
of adjoining chasm, not far from the bunker where
poor Burrows had been found frozen to the sand,
anyway according to my Uncle Jack.

'Hello there,' I cried in a muted fashion.

Fairbeat gave his well-timed wave.

Alfred's ball was either going to be found or not
found, so I walked over to the lonesome one.

'Still working on the flora, I hope.'

'Oh, yes.'

'Good show.' I paused, and a rush of fellow feeling
passed over me. 'I'm sure your botany's engrossing,
but wouldn't you like to play with a member
occasionally?'

'Oh, well . . .'

I took his hesitation as the unbridled enthusiasm of
a botanist, a foreign one at that.

'Let's talk about it back in the bar. There's a medal
coming up.'

'Do come on,' said Johnny Douglas. 'Just dig it out.'

'Coming, coming,' I cried back, and with a salute to
David Fairbeat said, 'See you later in the clubhouse.'

The round was much like any other, although of
course on the day it was unique, and we returned to
the clubhouse in good heart. I was getting my second

pint when I remembered Fairbeat. The Secretary was close by so I accosted him.

'Seen anything of Fairbeat recently?'

'Who?'

'The botanist.'

'The bottomist,' said Harry over his shoulder, a Parthian shot, as he made for the bar.

'Don't be so crass. He's a good fellow, just has his own interests.'

'Which don't include golf?' pursued Harry, turning round.

'Well, I think an inventory of the flora at St W's would be a good thing.' I felt determined.

'Oh yes,' said the Secretary. 'The botanist, of course. As a matter of fact I did take it up with the committee, and they're keen on the idea. The trouble is, I haven't since been able to track the botanist down.'

'He was playing today, for I chatted to him. In fact I'm surprised he's not in the bar.'

'He's an elusive fellow, that's for sure.'

'As befits a bottomist,' said Harry, with a heavy laugh.

'We've a reciprocal member, you know, who would interest you,' I said to a cheerful Celia over the buttered carrots.

'Reciprocal member? I thought you turned your noses up at that sort of thing. It's the sort of thing

Lake Park used to do. Not the great St Wilfrid's, surely?'

I pressed on regardless.

'A botanist, you know.'

She could not control an involuntary twitch of interest.

'Nice chap, though a bit introverted. He doesn't know anyone in the club yet, but I'm sure he soon will.'

'After his initiation, you mean?'

'Come, come, we're not like that.'

'Well, I'm sure his botany will bring him lots of friends.'

'I know what I'll do. We're playing the Clerihewists next Sunday, and I'll get Dickins to invite Fairbeat to play. He can't refuse. It's an affront to the club to have him playing on his own all the time.'

'Maybe he prefers to.'

'Pass the carrots, Celia.'

Dickins, after a twitch of his half-moons, did as he was asked and the normal request to play for the club was issued to Fairbeat. Dickins added in pen on my advice: 'You are expected to uphold the honour of the recip-rocals.'

This did the trick and Sunday week saw Fairbeat and myself third pair against the flower of the New Company of Clerihewists, though what became of the Old Clerihewists I know not.

'I'd like you to meet our new member, David Fairbeat, a fine golfer and an expert botanist.'

'Good show,' said the friendly Clerihewist. 'I've always had a bit of a penchant that way myself.'

So it proved.

'You'll find it just beyond the *Anagallis arvensis* or, as you'd know it, Jim, the Scarlet Pimpernel,' said the Clerihewist after Fairbeat turned his wrist over on the third and landed up close to the road.

'By Jove, I think you've found some *Veronica heredifolia*!' he cried when Fairbeat left it short and to the right at the fifth.

His partner joined in the fun.

'Veronica, eh? Leave some for me!'

'What on earth are they talking about?' I asked my partner.

He looked deeply grim and red.

'Ivy-leaved Speedwell is I believe the common name, eh, David?' shouted out the leading Clerihewist, but still Fairbeat was not to be drawn.

By the ninth my partner had clearly found it all too much. He had gained the fairway for once and I had put it on the green. Now he only had to put it close and we looked like getting one back.

The New Company of Clerihewists, however, were relentless.

'You must get a lot of *Montia perfoliata* round here?'

one of them asked as we closed on the green.

'A fair amount,' said my partner after a long pause.

'Of course, with the improved irrigation it may be failing somewhat.'

Like a man in a dream he replied after a further pause, 'Somewhat.'

It was all very annoying, particularly since my man left me six feet short and I missed the putt.

It was becoming increasingly clear that Fairbeat had no wish to trade metaphorical punches on the matter of our local flora and that his game was in pieces.

I tried to fight back. On the tenth I halted the older Clerihewist's swing.

'Steady on, old chap. I think that's a Surrey Skipper you're about to hit.'

'Don't be ridiculous, South, it's far too early in the year,' he said and proceeded to hit a beauty to the pin.

So we were roundly trounced.

Back in the clubhouse I took Fairbeat to one side. I'd really tried. I'd drawn him into club life and he had turned monosyllabic, cracked under pressure and, what was worse, had not even upheld the honour of the club when it came to the local flora.

'I mean to say, old chap, you might at least have won the wild flower conversation.'

I tried not to sound bitter.

At last he broke and the truth came out. In his

trembling voice he gave what I suppose you could call an explanation.

'You remember that day you came upon me?'

'Of course.'

'Well, I was enjoying myself.'

'Good.'

'Well, that's it.'

'What's it?'

'That is.'

'Let's get this straight. You were enjoying yourself, yes, but obviously you'd have enjoyed yourself more if you'd been playing with someone else.'

'No. Not obviously. Obviously not. In fact, you were the one who went on about wild flowers, simply because I happened to know the names of one or two.'

He then got quite heated.

'Golf is a wonderful game, a perfect test of skill, the supreme test of eye–hand–brain coordination, sustained over three or four hours. Why spoil it by having other people around?'

So there it was, all thrown back in my face, and I'd only tried to show a bit of goodwill to a new member.

Celia found it all very funny.

'He wasn't a botanist at all,' I told her disconsolately, 'he just liked playing on his own.'

'You should've let him be then, James.'

'But it's not the thing, Celia, it's not what a golf course is for.'

'I garden on my own, James.'
'Yes, but not to win.'
'Well, nor did your non-botanist.'
'Damned reciprocal, I'd say.'

Don't Send a Boy

'Do pick the damned thing up. You've had at least nine.'

He took another swing at it, and squirted it off into still longer grass. 'That's ten. For goodness' sake, you must pick it up.'

'I'm sure it's not.'

'I'm sure it is.'

Turning him to face the tee, I talked him through it.

'Off the tee onto the path. A mishit on the path. Three onto the fairway. Four into the rough on the right. Lost ball. Drop one, loss of one shot. I forgave you distance. Six into the dell short of the green. Seven over the back. Eight shanked into the bushes by the road. Nine an air shot. Ten you've just had.'

He looked puzzled.

'How many have you had, Uncle Jim?'

The rain was falling in a light mist across the links, bringing an early dusk to this February evening on which I had elected to indulge Freddy Junior's passion for the noble art. Cousin Freddy had asked us to have him for a weekend to calm him down as he made his final run-up to A-levels. 'A bit of quiet in the country will steady Fred's nerves,' Freddy Senior had said confidently. 'Blow the cotton wool out from between his ears.'

'Don't mind my score, old chap. Do you realise what time it is?'

'What time is it, Uncle?'

'Well past tea-time.'

'We've only played nine.'

'You've played nine on practically every hole.'

'I thought you wanted to encourage me.'

'I do, but you've got to take more of a grip, Fred. It's not just a question of whacking the ball.'

'But I love this game, Uncle. I always thought it was so dull when you and Dad played, but now I love it.'

The mist was thickening and moisture was seeping between my neck and collar. My hands were cold and my glove was at the stage just before soap.

'I really think we should go in, Fred. You look freezing.'

'If you like, Uncle,' he acquiesced, dragging his crest along the ground. A typical adolescent, adult one moment and child the next. Not the sort of person you want on a golf course.

'Oh well, I suppose we should press on, then,' I said, and his crest bobbed up as though it had never known a moment's doubt.

'Oh, I love this hole!'

The boy was obviously quite mad. The second, for we'd started on the tenth, is across an awkward series of hillocks up to a raised green surrounded by bunkers. The best play, surprisingly for St W's, is to be

152

long, for the bunkers are pigs, but you can play short into old man's valley and run up for a three and a half. I went for the heart and hit a beauty. It landed on the front right but then extraordinarily kicked further right, against the slope of the mound.

'Hard luck, Uncle. That was a great shot.'

'Thanks. See how you can do,' I said, with no great hope on his behalf.

Like the golfing gorilla, Shakespeare-style, this was his chance to prove the randomness of the universe, and this he duly did by putting the ball within three feet of the pin.

'Well played,' I said, with perhaps a touch of dismay in my voice.

'I told you I liked this hole. I knew we were right to go on.'

There's nothing more difficult than to show an act of kindness and then leave it unfinished, and I realised, with Fred's new enthusiasm unleashed by his last shot, that there was now no hope of tea.

As it happened, that was his last good shot of the round; unperturbed, he hacked on into the gathering gloom until the lights of the clubhouse beckoned like beacons and our round trudged to its dreary end.

To cap it all, Fred concluded by showing the true colours of the adolescent; he put his second at the eighth into the gorse, topped his fourth five yards and then hit a low hook into the long grass to the left of the fairway.

'Damn! Blast!' and suchlike punctuated this display, to be followed with, 'I really wish we had stopped at nine, Uncle. It's really too cold and dark.'

I didn't bother to reply but remarked inwardly on the burdens of fatherhood, and felt sorry for Freddy Senior. The final straw came back in the clubhouse. Fred was showering at excessive length and I was in need of some refreshment. At the bar I allowed my frustration to boil over. It was to a new member whom I didn't know, but he looked amiable enough.

'My goodness,' I said. 'Torment, sheer torment.'

'Oh yes?'

'Just torment.'

'And what, may I ask, constitutes the torment?'

'There is no torment greater than playing eighteen holes with a junior, even if he is your own blood.'

A deep frown crossed the man's hitherto vacant visage.

'That's a very sad thing to hear. You should realise there's no privilege greater than the fortune to play with your son.'

You get all sorts of members, even in a good club, especially in a good club, but I didn't feel I had to put up with this, least of all from a new member.

'Clearly not a man with a golfing son,' I said with a touch of acerbity.

'No, as a matter of fact,' and he pulled on his lager,

'I have three daughters,' adding with a smirk, 'and they're all single figures.'

'Well, my torment happens to be my nephew,' I retorted sharply and left to pull the torment out of the shower.

I didn't give Freddy Junior's golf another thought until Celia broke the news.

'Mother has invited us to stay in three weeks' time.'

'Oh.'

'I've spoken to Freddy, and they'll come over for dinner.'

'Fine.'

'Sadly, Freddy can't play golf with you, but Fred can.'

It was one of the conventions of a weekend with the Outlaw, as I thought of her, that I played golf with Freddy, who lived barely half an hour away in the distinguished county of Washire.

'That's a pity.'

'I thought you liked the boy.'

'I do, in a way, though at his age I can't say I saw the point in golf.'

'More interested in girls, weren't you?' she said in a surprisingly girlish way.

'Of course not,' I replied, disconcerted. 'Anyway, I like Fred.'

The truth is that I don't have much in common

with the younger generation, but I didn't want to put it so bluntly to the lady wife.

'It's just that I'll miss a good game with the dear cousin at Great Stonckley.'

'Well, Freddy has arranged a game for you with Robert Thorogood and son, so you won't miss your game on Saturday. And you can probably play with Fred on Sunday, too.' She added after a pause, 'So long as you're on good form on Saturday night. You know how Mother likes company.'

'I certainly do.'

Saturday morning rose windy and wet, with some promise of the weather clearing from the west. Freddy Junior arrived punctually, and although I appreciate the comfort and hospitality of the mother-in-law's abode – even if breakfast is frankly too large, with too much marmalade – my heart rose as I powered the jalopy out of the small drive and I could give my heart and soul to the matter in hand.

'We're meeting the Thorogoods up there,' I said to Fred by way of conversation.

I find with the younger generation that their heads are usually so heavy with confusion that a few self-evident remarks act to steady them.

'Thorogood's son can't play at all,' said Fred with feeling.

'Oh.'

'He's only about ten.'

We saw the Thorogoods in the car park at Stonckley, Robert with his unusual friendly grin and his boy's face small but shining.

'There's a medal, worse luck, but the pro says we can tee off from the eleventh if we're quick.'

Time spent in reconnaissance is never wasted, as the military have it, and Thorogood was clearly on top of things.

He continued, 'Follow me up the track beyond the practice ground, it's steep but firm. We'll go straight off from there.'

Bouncing through the beech woods, we reached a clearing to park in, almost at the top.

'Quick, they're coming down the tenth,' shouted Thorogood over the wind. The rain lashed against our faces.

'Come on, Fred, you'd better get moving,' I said.

With a scowl the lad got out, to see young Thorogood struggling bravely with the hatchback of his father's car.

'Quick, boys, run, faster! We mustn't get stuck behind the medal or we'll never get off.'

With my shoe-laces undone, still wearing my thin everyday socks and stumbling under the weight of my bag, I hurtled after Thorogood, with Fred panting fifteen yards behind me and Thorogood the younger puffing under his load even further back.

'We'll play a greensome!' Thorogood shouted.

'Fine,' I replied, though whether he heard in the wind I do not know. 'What's your boy off?' I added with a scream.

He showed no sign of having heard as we careered across the hillside on the mud and chalk path. At last we reached the eleventh tee. Through the lashing rain Thorogood cried, 'They're putting out on the tenth. It'd better be foursomes.'

'What shall we play for?' I asked.

'Is the green fee okay?'

'Fine,' I said. 'What's your boy off?'

'Just play. We can work out the handicap as we go.'

'Well, Fred's off twenty-four.'

Thorogood was concentrating on his shot, which he executed quite well, propelling the ball about 160 yards, low into the force-six wind. He looked up and said rather vaguely, 'Oh, about twenty-eight, I suppose.'

I always find it tough into a strong wind, despite my experience at St W's. There's always a tendency to overhit – not the wild lurch from the top of a youngster; more likely the pull as I strain for power. Anyway, that's what happened and the ball stopped in long grass about 120 yards from the tee. I wasn't helped by the panting frame of Fred arriving, succeeded as I completed my follow-through by an already exhausted young Thorogood.

'It's foursomes,' I said to Fred, who shrugged.

Thorogood waved at his boy, who unfortunately misunderstood and fumbled pathetically on the tee, searching for his ball.

'Come on, Alex,' shouted the father, 'it's foursomes.'

'What's that?' the boy replied, dismayed.

'You know,' his father shouted, 'alternate shots.'

The boy continued to fumble in his bag, water dripping off his nose.

'Come on, boy, they're leaving the tenth green.'

We set off at a trot.

Fred stamped about a bit in the long grass and I eventually found my drive. My young partner hit a surprisingly good five wood out of the rough and we made our way up to the Thorogood ball.

Young Alex looked down at it miserably. He had his feet very close together and swung freely three or four times, freely but without power.

'Get on with it,' said his father.

The boy took two more swings, closed on the ball and shanked it off into the long grass.

His father smiled weakly.

When they finally reached the broad, rolling green of the eleventh, Alex had put his father twice more into the rough and his father had hacked out, his weak smile being produced on each occasion.

'Putt out,' I said gallantly to young Alex.

'They're hitting their seconds. It's your hole,' said

his father, so we rushed onto the next.

'If I'm thirteen and Fred's twenty-four, and you're what, Robert? Ten? And Alex is twenty-eight, then we should play square,' I said as Fred took the tee. 'But all things considered, I think we should give you a shot on all the par fives.'

'Play on,' said Thorogood, 'they're hitting their thirds.'

'But are you happy with that?' I persisted.

'Fine, fine.' After a pause he added, 'Fine.'

Fred hit a pretty good six iron, but pulled. He left it in the rough above the hole, giving me quite a tricky pitch down onto the sloping green.

Alex stood bravely on the tee. Again he swung freely for a while.

His father encouraged him, 'Hurry up, Alex, they're putting out.'

He caught it thin, with an open face, and it squirted off about twenty yards down into thick gorse.

'Hard luck,' I said, but under my breath I was a little disheartened, if you see what I mean.

We rooted about a bit until Thorogood scooted back to play a third. He hit it up close to where we lay, but I pitched down, a real beauty, dead, and Alex whacked theirs off into gorse below the green.

'Your hole,' screamed Thorogood above the wind.

At the next tee I was prepared to be magnanimous; after all, it behoved me to make a game of it.

'A shot a hole on all but the par threes, I think, would be fair.'

'That's most generous,' said Thorogood with a note of resignation in his voice.

The thirteenth was a long par-four dogleg uphill. I hit a good one and so did Robert. As there was no sign of the medal I suggested, 'We might as well let the two boys drive as well. Let's make it a greensome, anyway.'

Fred hit a good one up the hill and Alex squirted one into the hawthorn, which can look quite attractive in bloom but in late March seemed dark and forbidding.

We were on in two, I hitting our second, and Alex skimming theirs ten yards forward from Thorogood's drive. Thorogood whacked it over the back. Alex thinned back down the hill, straight across the green, and Thorogood took masterly control. 'Your hole.'

'Three up, I think,' I said in friendly fashion. It was actually rather embarrassing, and to help keep the game alive I extended my magnanimity still further. 'A stroke a hole suit you?'

'That's very kind,' said Thorogood with still greater resignation.

At the long par five, our fourth, Alex hit a good approach shot and they got a six, net five, halving the hole. Then on top of the down, the wind screaming across from the English Channel, Robert's, Fred's and mine were all dragged away into the long grass to the right, while Alex, from the ladies' tee, managed to reach the fairway. The long grass could hide an elephant and had no trouble with our three balls.

Fred then took it into his head to lose all touch with the putter and, on the next, a par three, put us eight feet past from five feet, admittedly downhill.

More annoyingly, Robert played some great recovery shots and Alex's shanks, which occurred less frequently, didn't have the power to reach the rough.

So it was with some little amazement that we reached the first one down. I should say I was not at all down-hearted; I was glad to see the young men making a game of it.

We arrived at the first to a clear course.

'Couldn't we play a fourball?' asked Fred.

I was not against the idea, since it gave us a chance to renegotiate the handicaps. Thorogood was now being magnanimous, I think.

'Of course Fred should play his own ball, but I really don't think Alex is up to it.'

It was a point of view with which I could not disagree.

'Well, we'd better change the handicaps,' I said.

'God knows how,' said Thorogood.

Sitting down at home, quill in hand, it is of course easy to work it out. The beauty of golf is that there's always the correct handicap, if you have the mathematics to find it. But there, on that windswept down, with the wind and rain streaming across the rolling hills, my objectivity was weakened. All I was aware of was that we didn't deserve to be one down. And I was keen to make a game of it.

'You all take shots from me,' I offered.

'Stroke a hole, then, from both of you,' said Robert.

I thought for a moment.

'That doesn't sound right.'

'Why not?'

'Well, Fred is off twenty-four, so I should be giving him shots, which means you and Fred should be playing some level.'

'Yes, but you've got two balls against our one.'

'Yes, but you're playing a greensome.'

It was truly confusing, particularly since no one could be said to be playing to handicap. The impasse was broken by the shivering figure of the small Thorogood.

'What are you talking about, Dad?'

'Oh, we're just having fun,' replied Thorogood père.

Clearly we had to resolve the matter before exposure set in, so I offered a stroke a hole from myself, and a stroke on all but the par threes from Fred.

'Fine,' said Thorogood. His voice had lost the resignation I had noted earlier; it was almost steely.

Unfortunately we didn't get the handicaps quite

right. Fred played ever more wildly and they hung onto their lead. Representative of the second ten was the seventh. I was in the thorn, but Fred hit a good drive and was on the green in three. Robert's drive was excellent. Alex squared up nervously for the second. He was 210 across the wind. He took an enormous swipe and missed. I thought the boy would cry. In his exasperation he prepared to take another swipe.

Thorogood was as quick as a flash.

'No, old chap, leave it. Anyway, it was a much better shot than shanked into the bushes.'

A rather cutting remark, I thought, but undoubtedly true.

Thorogood then took his driver and hit a beaut. When we reached the green we saw that it had been over-beauted, for it lay over the back.

'Hard luck, Robert,' I said. 'That was a great blow.'

We were looking good, but in classic schoolboy style Alex chipped dead, the only time on the round, and the hole was theirs.

'Good chap,' I said to the shivering boy.

'Don't forget his second, either,' said his father, putting his arm around the boy's shoulders.

I parted with twenty pounds in the car park with reasonable grace. I couldn't quite work out how we had lost, but we were all so wet that I didn't give it much thought.

★

In a hot bath back at the Outlaw's I mused, with peripheral irritation, that handicapping – the great glory of golf, the perfect leveller not open to tennis, squash, cricket, chess, you name it – worked only with some predictability, if the handicappees played to some level of consistency. And consistency was the one thing you could not expect from the young. Keep them at arm's length, I thought to myself.

I lazed away in the comfort of the well-fitted bathroom, fully in keeping with the pleasant decor of the Outlaw's Tudor home. New Tudor, of course, and very nice too. But my physical comfort was spoiled by the conundrum of the proper handicapping for our day's golf. Perhaps I wouldn't have been so concerned if I'd won.

This inner dialogue had coincided with idle probing up the cold tap by the big toe of my right foot. It was an ignominious figure who cried out to Celia for help. By the time olive oil was administered, amidst fits of girlish giggles, on the advice of the Outlaw (though not, you'll be relieved to hear, in her presence), the unpredictability of the young had been driven from my mind. Over dinner, however, the subject re-emerged.

'Don't worry, Tish,' I said to Freddy's wife. 'Once young Fred finds out about girls he'll forget golf for a while.'

'Oh, do you think so, Jim?' asked Celia with amusement.

'I wish you were right, but not any more, I fear,' said Tish. 'The next generation seems golf-mad, even the girls.'

'How terrible,' said Celia's mother.

'I agree,' said Cousin Freddy. 'A young man should be playing rugger, or football. Only old men get obsessed by golf.'

'Really, Freddy, I don't think Jim's old, are you, dear? Limping a bit, perhaps, but hardly old.'

I could see that Celia was about to tell the story of the toe-in-tap débâcle, so I went to the kitchen. I returned to find that the conversation had made little progress.

'Just wait, Freddy,' said Celia. 'Once young girls start playing golf they'll take over the courses, just you watch.'

'They are already. You may not realise it, Jim, but Fred's girlfriend is a keen golfer.'

'And not much good, either,' rejoined Fred.

'Always the mark of a keen golfer,' I offered.

'Jim,' said Tish, 'if you had a son, you'd teach him golf, wouldn't you?'

'Really, Tish, what a thought! The question simply doesn't arise,' I said.

'Yes, but if the question did arise?' asked Freddy, seeing, no doubt, the chance for some family humour.

I stuck to my guns. 'Well, it doesn't.'

Celia's mother joined in. 'Answer the question, Jim.'

'I haven't really thought.'

Tish persisted. 'Well, while you're not thinking, what would you do if it was a girl?'

'In that case the question really doesn't arise, since it would be a matter for Celia.'

This made everyone laugh a lot, especially Celia.

Dinner passed peacefully to a close, as it does, and over our farewells I attempted to confirm golf for the following morning with Freddy but he was otherwise engaged. 'Celia told you I can't play, I hope, but Fred's eager to have another go.'

'Fine,' I said, my avuncular role seemingly unavoidable.

'Come round at about nine. You should get off all right as a single tomorrow.'

Nine o'clock duly saw me on the steps of Freddy's spacious country house.

'I'm here for Fred,' I said to the cleaning lady who met me at the door and let me in.

'You'll be lucky,' she replied somewhat curtly, closing the door behind me.

'He's supposed to be up at nine to play golf.'

'It would be more than my life's worth to wake him,' she said with passion.

'Is anyone else awake?'

'Mr Freddy's long since gone, and Mrs South is breakfasting in bed.'

At that moment there was a firm knock on the front
door, and the cleaning lady opened it again.

'Hello, Jane, is Fred up?'

'You'd better join the queue, dearie. This gentleman's before you.'

'I'm his uncle,' I interjected, trying to establish my
standing.

'Oh, Uncle Jimbo? How lovely! I've always wanted
to meet you.'

I looked at the young lady rather more carefully. She
had rather décolletée flowing garments, long hair and
a powerful jaw, but was not bad-looking, really.

My gaze was obviously misinterpreted, for she
rapidly continued, 'Don't worry, I'm Fred's girlfriend.'

'Oh, how nice,' I said. 'Actually, I've come over to
play a round of golf with Fred. Perhaps you'd like to
walk round with us?'

She frowned slightly, rather in the way Sammy, my
old tennis partner, used to. Like Sammy, she was also
well built. The frown hovered a moment, until she gave
her head a little shake and, smiling brightly, said, 'I
play golf myself, you know.'

At that moment we heard crashing from above and
Fred appeared at the top of the stairs.

'Hi, Uncle! Ready to go?'

'Certainly, but there's someone else here for you.'

'Oh, Natalie, great! Do you want to walk round with
us?'

'Oh, Fred, I can't manage it. But,' and she produced an even more powerful smile, 'I couldn't just come up for a moment, could I? There's something I must ask you about.'

That was it, as it turned out. Clearly she had a quite a bit to talk about, serious stuff, apparently, for it was almost eleven by the time she came downstairs again. Seeing me still waiting at the breakfast table, she smiled most sweetly.

'I just *had* to talk to Fred. I'm so sorry to have kept you waiting.'

'Not at all,' I said gallantly. 'Is he on his way down?'

'Oh, I do hope so, for your sake, though I'm awfully afraid he may have fallen asleep again.'

'That's a pity,' I said feebly.

She looked rather crestfallen.

'I fear it doesn't look as if you'll get your game, Mr South.' She thought deeply for a moment. 'I know, why don't you play a threeball with Fred and me this afternoon?'

The idea rather took me by surprise.

'Sadly, my wife and I have to drive back this afternoon,' I explained.

'Oh, what a shame. Some other time, then,' she said with a really glowing smile.

It struck me again how much she was like Sammy, the girl of my youth.

★

On the drive back I told Celia about Fred's failure to surface. She seemed most amused, though as it turned out she had other things on her mind.

'I'm so glad you enjoy playing with the young.'

'Yes, I suppose I do once in a while.'

'I never thought you had much interest in it before.'

'Well, I can't say I have that much interest now,' I said with a laugh.

'But you do have some interest, don't you?'

'Oh yes, some interest.'

'I'm so glad,' she said, and she put her hand on my knee as I navigated the roundabout and we left the M25.

I rather left it at that, but it was only with the passing of time that the full significance of it came to me. I'm sure you'll blush for me as I recount the conversation over breakfast two months later.

Celia was just clearing away and I remarked casually, 'By the way, dear, don't you think you're putting on a bit of weight?'

'It's hardly surprising, Jim.'

Well, you've guessed the rest.

It interrupted my summer's golf a little, but fortunately my games with Fred and Alex had already got me over the psychological hurdle of playing golf with the young and I could contemplate the future with a steady nerve.

The Old Heave-ho

I felt the merest bat's squeak in my left shoulder-blade as I picked up the clubs and carried them through the hall to my car. I gave my neck a little turn, flexed my shoulders in an athletic kind of way and, with a spring in my stride, made for my gallant jalopy. It was a medal morning.

When I took up position at the wheel the bat's squeak returned, still inaudible except to the trained ear, and I shifted my torso. It was the sort of quiver, more an itch than a stab of pain, that tenses even the finely tuned body of an Olympic competitor, and although in middle age I felt somewhat short of that, I was not at all out of condition.

'Have a lovely game, Jim,' shouted Celia from the porch. 'And don't forget to pick those things up from the Sandersons.'

'What things?'

'You know, I told you; the baby things, the cot. You know.'

'Oh yes, of course.' But then I hesitated. 'Who exactly are the Sandersons?'

'Oh, Jim, really! They've lived down by Swallow's Mill for years.'

'Yes, yes.' I did sort of remember. 'They don't play golf, I think.'

'You know very well they don't. And they're a charming couple,' she added, with menace.

'Ah well.' I sighed. 'Ah well.'

'Please don't annoy me, James.'

I went back, leant across Celia's growing tummy and gave her a peck on the cheek. Then, with a cheery, 'I'll be back at about six,' I was off.

The day's anticipation was still keen, but those domestic thoughts had endangered the inner calm, or karma as I believe it's called, that is essential to the hunter of the links.

I raised my right arm to pull down the seat belt and the bat gave another yelp. I rolled my head again, only to release another yelp a little lower down my shoulder, closer to the centre of my spine. Uh-huh, I said to myself. A small muscular discomfiture is the very thing, on a medal morning like today, to urge enough restraint to avoid the greatest golfing error, namely overswinging from an excess of athleticism.

By the time I reached St W's, however, I had jiggled about enough in my driving seat to establish quite definitely that I had an incipient strain. My neck was stiff and both my shoulders seemed to be squeaking in unison as I lifted out my golf bag and began to walk up the steps to the clubhouse.

'You look a bit under the weather,' said Johnny Douglas in his friendly way as I reached the putting green. 'Something wrong with your neck?'

'It's my shoulders, actually.'

'Tell me about it,' he said and, picking up his ball, went off to join Bob, already wreathed in pipe smoke, on the first tee.

It was perfectly all right for Johnny to assume this studied indifference, for I knew the medal prize was as good as mine.

When he saw me contorting myself in the changing-room, trying to pull on my golf shirt without intensifying the rick, Alfred said, 'A wounded golfer, eh? Nothing so dangerous as a wounded golfer, they say.'

'They do indeed say,' I replied to our distinguished accountant. 'And damned painful it is, too.'

'What, the neck?'

'No, the way they always say the same thing.'

'Well, it's true.'

'It may be true, but it's a damned nuisance.'

'I'm sorry if I've upset you,' said Alfred with perhaps the merest whiff of sincerity.

'You're not upsetting me, it's my shoulder.'

'I thought you said it was your neck.'

'No, you said it was my neck.'

Alfred sighed deeply, buckled his belt and said decisively, 'If you're well enough to play, we're off in ten minutes.'

I grunted a reply. Of course I was well enough to play. It was a typical wind-up remark from an old dog of the sandy track.

I played like a dream. The only time I faltered was at the seventeenth when, six better than my handicap, I strolled onto the tee and remarked to Alfred, 'I think the strain has completely gone.'

'You're facing disaster here, then.'

'I don't think so,' I said calmly.

On the tee I swung freely for the first time that round. The wind was steady from the south-west, the proper wind for the course, and my normal play on this longish par three was to hit a low three iron the required 200 yards. Rather a chicken shot, to be truthful, since I was almost always short, but short was fine. It would give me a low-running chip, which might get close enough for my par, while not having endangered my tee shot with the pot bunkers to the left or the long stuff up by the green on the right.

But today it was different.

'I think I'll fade a drive into the wind and drop it safely onto the right-hand part of the green, to let it run down to the hole.'

'Like hell,' said my churlish partner.

He was out of it, having taken a nine at the eleventh, so his chagrin was to be expected, I suppose, though I don't think it did him any credit.

I swung freely and caught the ball cleanly. My body weight came through and the ball soared off the face of the club. Sadly, the doom-laden prognostications of Alfred Dickins were borne out. The freedom of my swing encouraged me to come back too far at the backswing, so that the rhythm was temporarily misplaced. My hands felt the urge to catch up my sliding hips, causing my shoulder to rotate too fast, eventually not giving my hips time to clear. You may think this all sounds rather technical, but the truth is that with a bit of thought any of us could be a first-rate coaching pro – or, anyway, a second-rate one. In any event, the result was a huge, raking hook onto the tenth fairway.

'Damn it.'

'Predictable.'

I didn't bother to reply, but strode off after the ball with some hauteur. When I reached it I was relieved to find, as I lowered my bag, that the temporary suspension of the shoulder strain had ended. My confidence flowed back and, with a strain-restricted nine iron, I flighted the ball into the welcoming embrace of the seventeenth green.

Par was not to be mine, but even so the hole was no disaster, and I strode into the clubhouse lord of all I surveyed. I had won the medal. I must admit, I did hang around for a while in front of the scoreboard. It did look awfully good, a net sixty-five.

The gods must have laughed, as they laughed at Pyrrhus after yet another disastrous victory. Actually, I suspect those Roman gods spent most of their time laughing, and when the modern world took over and things got rather serious – march of civilisation, progress and all that – I think those old gods took up residence on golf courses and cried their eyes out in uncontrollable mirth.

'A good hot bath's all you need,' said Celia when I got home, struggling with the baby gear from the Sandersons.

Personally I like a hot bath, and the strain in my shoulder was ample excuse.

'And when you're out I'll rub some embrocation into it.'

What it is to have a loving wife and mother-to-be!

As it happened, I fell into the first trap of hot bath-manship; I stayed in about thirty seconds too long. I came out with my brain boiled and my feet swollen. I was a little overcooked for the embrocation.

Perhaps my slight sharpness to the lady wife – 'Don't rub too hard' – was a mistake, or maybe I was too inviting a target for wifely affection, but anyway, by the time I got down to dinner, my shoulder was really stiff and my neck was moving with the freedom of a rhino's.

'If there's something really the matter, you should see the doctor,' said Celia as I leant across the table for the butter and winced at the searing pain.

'Don't be silly, dear. He'll just bounce me onto some damned physio, from quack to quack. They're no different from golf professionals.'

'I've never heard of one golf professional recommending another one.'

'You're absolutely right. Pros don't gang up against you like quacks do.'

I cut a piece of Camembert. It tasted chalky.

'You are in a bad mood, Jim. I thought you said you'd won the medal.'

'I did. That's why I need to see the pro.'

'I think Dr Jebbins would be a good idea, you know.'

'I should think Jebbins has had a surfeit of the South family complaints as it is.'

'Pregnancy is not a complaint, dear. A badly strained shoulder is.'

'Don't let's talk about it. I'm touched by your interest, but I'm sure it will be better in the morning.'

I was, but it wasn't.

In my heart I know I'm not the world's best patient – inclined to exaggerate the seriousness of my own malady, but disinclined to take decisive action to remedy it – so it was that, despite the sharp pains that punctuated my sleep with each shift of my torso, I left the house the following morning to earn an honest crust with my head veering off at an angle that was anything but jaunty.

The condition was so obvious that, even as I let slip

to my golf-infatuated colleagues that I'd won the medal, news normally designed to elicit a snarl, this Monday it elicited nothing but laughter.

'And paid the ultimate price, by the look of it,' was one rather representative remark.

The week was a torture, but a gradually diminishing one, and by Saturday I was once more ready to swing the misshapen implement of golf.

Foursomes are the finest version of golfing competition. Hitting alternate shots, so that you never hit your own ball, but always your partner's, puts exquisite pressure on the golfer beyond that awful torment he puts on himself. It is an extraordinary dual pressure, partly from your opponents but also from your partner, whom you are probably more eager to please than yourself. And then the added, final cut comes from the well-chosen word that can sow dissension in even the most battle-hardened team of veterans.

It is sometimes said that the decline in foursomes golf arises from the growing selfishness of the average club golfer. I'm afraid it is rather due to the decline of moral fortitude.

And that Saturday my partner had to show all the moral fortitude available. As it happened, I was playing a friendly with Harry the humorist against Johnny and Bob.

Harry threw a tee in the air and it fell pointing roughly at our opponents.

'Off you go, then. Age before beauty.'

Harry was the oldest and had lost most of his hair, so he thought he was entitled to make remarks like this.

Bob hit a steady ball, slightly drawn, into the middle of the fairway. For once there only the merest zephyr to disturb the early autumnal mist.

'Well, master of the medal, lead off the good guys.'

Harry was determined to keep the conversational initiative. He had seized the clichéd high ground and did not intend to let it go.

His wit did nothing to help me. The damp morning was gnawing at my shoulder, plucking the taut violin strings that ran from my neck to the inner cords of my spinal column. I took a few practice swings.

'You look awkward today,' said Johnny.

'No barracking from our opponents,' said Harry. 'In any event, there's nothing more dangerous than a wounded golfer.'

Whether it was this remark that proved the last straw, or I was close to breaking naturally, I don't know, but I went to the tee in trepidation.

I was determined not to overswing – I had, after all, at least another forty shots to play – but there is a limit to how short your swing can be and still generate clubhead speed. I was well beyond the limit, or not up to it, if you see what I mean. I played and the ball left the tee, gathered some height, but stopped after about fifty yards in the rough.

'Rather deliberate, old chap,' said Harry, probably trying to goad me into a bit more swing.

'Underswinging is one thing but that was ridiculous,' said Bob, in my view going beyond what is acceptable, even in foursomes.

I picked up my tee, to a sharp twang in my left shoulder, and commented, 'Just loosening, just loosening.'

'Keep it up,' said Johnny.

Harry hit a pretty good one from the rough, and I poked it up towards the green with some success, but no lessening of the stiffness.

At the second Harry put it firmly on the green and I putted well to level the scores. My drive at the third was again short but not quite so painful, and we made our merry way round. I was playing at half-strength, not exactly helping Harry much, but not destroying our chances.

On the sixth Harry hit a beauty, giving me a reasonable chance to go for the green in more normal circumstances.

'Do you mind? I think I'll just prod it up short of the bunkers,' I said.

'Rather windy,' said Johnny.

Harry obviously agreed and, to my mind rather foolishly, commented, 'We don't want to see our partner strain himself, do we?'

The truth is that our partner, namely me, was badly strained and they had been very lucky I'd been prepared to make up the four. Harry's remark continued to rankle, and Bob took advantage of it on the ninth. The wind had got up, though of course there's always a wind at Wilfrid's, and with a really good drive the green could be reached.

'Going for the green, eh?' asked Bob.

'Of course he's not,' said Harry, another mistake on his part.

'Of course I am,' said I.

It was foolish, I grant you, but my patience was exhausted, not just with my opponents and my partner, but most of all with the gnawing pains in my neck and shoulders.

The result was inevitable. As Harry positioned himself above the long dune grass, trying to avoid toppling over as he hit our second twenty yards on from the tee where I had topped it, I realised that I had not just thrown caution to the winds, but with it lost any hope for a short-term recovery of my severely strained back.

I limped on but by the fifteenth it was all over, five and three. 'What shall we play for on the bye?' asked Johnny smugly.

'I don't think my partner's up to it,' Harry riposted.

'Actually, I've got to agree. I'll walk in.'

They looked at me with sympathy, with pity and, I realised, with growing condescension. I was to become familiar with all three sentiments over the next few months.

'Hard cheese, old boy,' said Harry, but he was obviously pleased to see the back of me, an attitude not entirely dispelled when they joined me over the foaming in the bar.

'Well, Jim, I suppose you'll be in hospital next week,' cracked Johnny in his insensitive way.

'I certainly won't. It's just a little crick.'

'Just a little something else, I'd say,' said Harry venomously.

On other occasions I might have been rather amused to see Harry's raucous sense of humour reduced to this thin childish snarl, but I have to admit that the pain in my neck, which now spread almost to my waist, was a bit of a humour handicap.

The best bitter did not improve my mood. Not prolonging the agony, I made my way gingerly down the steps to my car. Harry's words rang in my ear.

'Better see a quack, old boy.'

I now started on a period of my life that I hope never to relive. I began to envy Job.

Dr Jebbins was true to form.

'Aye,' he said, looking into the distance over his half-moon spectacles. 'Aye. Your shoulder, you say? Aye. And how's Mrs South? Fine woman, fine woman.'

'Celia's very well, thank you.'

'A difficult time, pregnancy.' He stared even further into the distance. 'Aye.'

Jebbins was the last of the old breed, the country GP *par excellence*. His surgery was like a schoolmaster's study and I entered with the same non-specific sense of guilt.

'I can promise you, Doctor, that there's no connection between my shoulder and my pregnancy.'

'Mrs South's, you mean.'

'Quite.'

'Aye.'

We had a moment of silence.

'Well, then, if it's a physio you want, a physio you shall have.'

'Thank you, Doctor.'

'My pleasure, my plesure.'

'Just lie on your front with your face in this hole. That's it. Now put your arms by your side, good, and relax. Good.'

I had climbed onto the plasticated slab masquerading as a physiotherapy couch, and now the indignity was well advanced. I had kept my trousers firmly in place, but I still felt naked under the survey of the masterful masseuse – or highly trained physiotherapist, by any other name.

'A little awkward here, so?' she asked, driving her witch's fingers into my shoulder-blade.

'Aaagh!'

'Good . . . And here?'

'*Aaagh!*'

'Good . . . And here?'

I was speechless. Even if my back had been a purring trampoline of well-tensioned fibres, her brutal attentions might have produced a muffled gasp. As it was, I quivered like a jelly. Anyone would have done so.

Up to that moment I had always considered a massage as being a somewhat self-indulgent extension of the hot bath. I was soon educated.

To add to the physical misery there was the sheer torture she inflicted at the conclusion of each session.

'And don't forget, Mr South,' she said, a ludicrous grin like a chimpanzee's spreading from ear to ear, 'don't forget, absolutely no golf at all, not even one little hole.'

After my third visit, as I returned to Celia a whimpering cur, I tried to be positive, turning my shoulders rather than my neck, which was in a rigid position in the brace with which the physio had fixed me up.

'I suppose it might be worse. She might be sticking pins in me.'

'It's surprising you should say that, Jim, but Margaret, you know, one of the other mothers at the maternity classes, said that you should try acupuncture.'

'Great, that's all I need.'

'Only if Mrs Shelburne doesn't do the trick.'

'Mrs Hellburn, you mean.'

'She's meant to be very good, you know.'

'If she was any good, I'd be back on the course by now.'

'These things take time, James. After all, it was too much golf that caused the problem in the first place.'

'Don't be ridiculous, Celia. I've played golf for years and I've never been off for even a week before.'

Celia looked thoughtful, and I could see that she was trying to decide whether to let the matter drop, but there's a brave, foolhardy side to her.

'Funnily enough, Jim, we were discussing that, too.'

'What?'

'Well, you're not the only husband having troubles.'

'*What?*'

She should have stopped there, really.

'Well, Margaret's husband has swollen right out.'

'That's ridiculous,' I spluttered. 'You can't be suggesting . . .'

'Only his ankles, of course, not his tummy.'

'Well, that's all right, then,' I said and left, in an awkward kind of way, to watch the evening news on television.

It was three weeks later that I had my first acupuncture session.

187

I am, of course, familiar with the mysteries of the Orient, my game of skins proved that, but the childish theory that localised pain in one part of the anatomy will generate sympathetic healing in another – banging your head on a brick will also cure stomach-ache – is plainly ridiculous. I know that, but Celia had caught me at a weak moment, over the breakfast table.

'If you really wanted to get better, you'd at least consider it.'

I gazed miserably at the slice of toast as I crushed the hard butter into it. I had given up muesli in favour of a gentleman's breakfast, so desultory were my opportunities for pleasure.

'You don't have to be a fully paid-up Buddhist, you know, to give it a try.'

I scooped the thick-cut marmalade onto the side of the plate, dropping a chunk onto a bit of the Sunday papers. There was no hurry, even though it was the morning of the monthly medal.

'I might pop up to the club before lunch, just to see how they're getting on.'

'If you like,' said Celia in a non-commital way.

In the midst of this prolonged agony, little Johnny South entered the world. I won't take you through it blow by blow; suffice it to say that being present during the great process of birth, even in the furthest chair, by the door, is worse than seeing one's partner frozen over a three-footer to win the club's mixed four-somes. Not so much for the intensity of the mental agony, but for how long it goes on. It's not so special for the lady, either.

Still, pain is a bonding process and mother nature takes no prisoners. As for bonding with my son, even as I regarded that tiny frame, those fingers the size of tees, I tried to imagine the youth, three iron in hand, squaring up to go for the green at the sixth, wind against. The picture did not come easily, and I resolved that bonding would have to wait.

I could, however, play the father's part, and despite my continued enforced absence from the links, I thought I owed it to the boys to wet young South's head, and this I duly did. It gave me another welcome excuse to visit the club.

'Mine's a large Scotch,' said Bob.

'The same,' said Harry.

'What did you say the boy's name was?' asked Johnny Douglas.

'Johnny.'

'Good name, good name. I'll have the same.'

It was only on my way home that I considered what a strange spectacle I must have made. Not playing, but imposing on my erstwhile partners contemplation of hearth and home, kinder and küche. Soon I'd be talking to them of kirche. It's surprising how insensitive one can be, how quickly one can lose touch.

Celia was out of hospital in no time at all. Naturally I offered to help as much as I could, but the arrival of the Outlaw lessened the need. I have to say that my mind was largely dominated by that other big event in my life, my back.

Celia's mother didn't help with her homely wisdom.

'Don't worry, Jim. As soon as Celia's up and about you'll be fine.'

But it was not to be. Autumn passed into winter, winter into spring. Johnny began to be weaned, but my back made no progress. Acupuncture gave way to aromatherapy, aromatherapy to psychic healing, psychic healing to experiments with diet, from no meat to all meat, no trace minerals to iron-and-zinc-enriched. I even contemplated mass hypnotism by a cult of Taoist monks. It was not to be. My back and shoulders conspired with my neck to make me a sad victim of the modern world.

It all came to a head over dinner, with the Sandersons of all people. Welsh, by origin, they had a way with words.

'You used to be a golfer, didn't you, Jim?' asked Jane Sanderson.

'I still am,' I said.

'Oh,' replied Jane, gazing at my neck brace.

Derek Sanderson coughed and said, 'Can I help with the dishes, Celia?'

I tried to rise and Celia put her hand gently on my shoulder.

'Don't worry, Jim.'

'Ever thought of taking up the game yourself?' I asked Derek when he returned from the kitchen.

'It's too dangerous for me, I'm afraid.'

'Really, Derek, that's not very funny,' said Jane.

This conversation ran through my head that night as I lay on my back on the heated wooden board that passed for a bed. They were right. Tactless as they were, I was not a golfer any more.

The next morning I told Celia my decision.

'By the way, dear, I'm going to see the Secretary.'

'That's nice.'

'Yes.' I reached for another piece of toast, with some pain. After a gulp of coffee, I continued, 'There's not much point in being a member if you can't play.'

Celia looked thoughtful, but little Johnny had started to cry and needed feeding.

'What a shame, dear.'

It had been some time since I'd been up to the club, but I could have driven there blindfold.

'Nice to see you, Mr South,' the Steward said in greeting. 'Keeping well?'

'Not particularly. Is the Secretary around?'

'You'll find him in the usual place.'

I found the young fellow filling out handicap returns. My mission was the work of a few moments.

'There's no point in beating about the bush. I've decided to resign from the club.'

'Are you sure, Mr South? You know there's a very long waiting list.'

'I'm sure.'

Perhaps I choked a bit. When you're speaking with a ramrod back and your neck in a brace it is not easy to sound natural.

'Well then, I'll inform the committee. They will be disappointed.'

He shook my hand firmly, causing me to wince, and the deed was done.

It only remained to bury the corpse, and this I hoped to achieve by a visit to the pro's shop at Lake Park. I couldn't bring myself to stay any longer at St Wilfrid's.

'They've served me well,' I said to Arnie the professional. 'Find them a good home.'

Arnie primped his coiffure. 'They're very outdated, Mr South. I don't know if I'll be able to shift them at all.'

'They've seen their moments, you know. Great moments.'

'There's no market for an old set like this. Why not try the antiques shop?'

I suppose that was meant to be funny but I didn't rise to the occasion.

'Or Oxfam, perhaps?' continued the junior pro, practising the light wit that is so much part of the golf professional's trade.

I left Lake Park with both my clubs and my dignity. A burial at sea, or anyway the local canal, seemed the only fitting end, and this I duly executed. I was aware that this was not exactly ecological, so I had to wait until there were no cars in sight. When finally I committed the bag and clubs to the deep, they made a somewhat disappointing splash.

Dinner that night with Celia was not a success, and even Johnny seemed down in the mouth. I went to bed, my lonely hard board, after one whisky too many, with a heavy heart. A whole chapter of my life had been consigned to the local canal. I was a golfer no more. I had crept off the stage of golf, the stage of life, or so it felt. And as I lay in bed that night I could hear the sniggers of those classical gods; another human being bereft, his dreams turned to ashes.

I suppose the next morning must have been red-nose day on Mount Olympus; their tears of mirth must have been running like streams down those crags. For I woke the next morning to a new world. The morning chorus roused me as usual, and I turned myself gingerly over to switch on the light. No pain.

No pain? I lay still. I tried to recall the events of the previous day: the firm handshake of the Secretary, the sickening splish of the clubs in the canal. It all came back to me. I sat up and moved my neck. No pain! I got off the board and jumped in the air. No pain! I ran downstairs, almost knocking over Johnny's pram. I ran into the street. I ran back into the house and bumped into Celia coming out. I hugged her, I picked her up, I twirled her round. No pain!

Then I went into the sitting-room, sat down and burst into tears.

'Why don't you take up cricket?' suggested Celia.